ACTION RESEARCH:
A GUIDE FOR LIBRARY MEDIA SPECIALISTS

Jody K. Howard
Su A. Eckhardt

Linworth
PUBLISHING, INC

Your Trusted
Library-to-Classroom Connection.
Books, Magazines, and Online.

Library of Congress Cataloging-in-Publication Data

Howard, Jody K.
　Action research : a guide for library media specialists / Jody K. Howard, Su A. Eckhardt.
　　　p. cm.
　Includes bibliographical references and index.
　ISBN 1-58683-177-1 (pbk.)
　1. School libraries—Research—Methodology. 2. Instructional materials centers—Research—Methodology 3. Action research. 4. Action research in education. I. Eckhardt, Su A. II. Title.
Z675.S3H6775 2005
027.8—dc22
　　　　　　　　　　　　2004023203

Table of Contents

Table of Figures v

Acknowledgments vi

Introduction ix

Chapter 1 Stepping Into Action Research 1
    The Why of Action Research 1
    School Improvement and Accountability 2
    The What of Action Research 2
    Reflective Practice 3
    Action Research Versus Traditional Research 3
    Advantages and Disadvantages of Action Research 4
    The Action Research Spiral 6
    Action Research Scenario 7
    Chapter Summary 7

Chapter 2 Exploring the Topic 9
    Selecting the Topic 9
    Reviewing the Literature 12
    Chapter Summary 17

Chapter 3 Assessing the Environment 19
    The Community 19
    The School 21
    The Library 23
    Chapter Summary 27

Chapter 4 Problem Statement to Research Question 28
    Developing the Problem Statement 28
    Developing the Research Question 32
    Chapter Summary 34

Chapter 5 Collecting Data 35
    Data Collection Tools 35
    Questionnaires 36
    Interviews 40
    Observations 42
    Archival Information 44
    Chapter Summary 44

Chapter 6 Planning Considerations	45
Generalizability	45
Validity	46
Reliability	46
Personal Bias	47
Personal Ethics	48
Timeline	48
Peer Review	49
Chapter Summary	50
Chapter 7 Organizing and Interpreting Data	51
Coding the Data	51
Analysis of Data	54
Chapter Summary	56
Chapter 8 Finalizing the Action Research	57
Spiraling Into the Future	57
Assessment of the Plan	61
Chapter Summary	63
Chapter 9 Sharing with Colleagues	65
Sharing Locally	66
Sharing at Conferences	69
Publishing in Professional Journals	71
Chapter Summary	74
A Final Word	75
Appendix 1 Contact Information for Journals	77
Appendix 2 Sample Project for Publication	81
Appendix 3 Web Resources for Action Research	95
Appendix 4 Recommended References	99
Works Cited	105
Glossary	107
Index	111
About the Authors	113

Table of Figures

Figure 1.1 Traditional Versus Action Research — 4

Figure 1.2 Advantages and Disadvantages of Action Research — 5

Figure 1.3 The Spiral of Action Research — 6

Figure 2.1 Literature Review Graphic Organizer — 15

Figure 2.2 Megan's Literature Review Graphic Organizer — 16

Figure 3.1 Areas to Explore in Projects — 26

Figure 5.1 Triangulation Matrix — 35

Figure 5.2 Advantages and Disadvantages of Questionnaires — 38

Figure 5.3 Advantages and Disadvantages of Interviews — 41

Figure 5.4 Advantages and Disadvantages of Observations — 43

Figure 5.5 Megan's Data Collection Sources — 44

Figure 8.1 Megan's Plan — 61

Acknowledgments

We have been assisted and supported with this book by a great many friends, colleagues, and family members both individually and as a team. These we do now gratefully acknowledge.

Shared Acknowledgments

Together, we would like to thank our encouragers and supporters including Keek Hill, "our Megan," whose action research project we have adapted throughout the manuscript; Robin Jones who shared her action research project to be included in our book; Wendy Isaacs a "random airplane lady" from Bristo Middle School who gave us her thoughts, questioned us, and generally shared her middle school experiences during an airplane flight to a conference; Gina Flores for excellence in spiral building and tiff instructions; and our students and friends for sharing their real-life experiences.

We would also like to thank Donna Miller for her encouragement to write and publish this body of work; and Sherry York, our editor, who worked long and hard to help us refine our manuscript into a professional product.

Jody's Acknowledgments

Many years ago, I was talking to my father, Richard F. Howard, about writing a book and he shared with me his desire to write also. Unfortunately, he passed away before he was able to act upon this dream. I thank him for fostering in me a similar desire to find a passion and then to write about this passion. I would also like to thank my wonderful sons, Joe and Will, for listening to me talk incessantly about this subject that I find so interesting. And, this project could not have been a success without the collaborative sessions with my wonderful friend, Su, who is able to clarify so much which could have been incomprehensible without her perceptive ability.

Su's Acknowledgments

My personal thank you goes to my wonderful and infinitely patient husband, Randy, for his support, giving up our time together, and thoughtful ability to see the book's purpose while developing our glossary of terms; my daughter, Kris, for understanding the importance of this effort and volunteering to cook and do the washing when I could not, due to the demands of writing and editing; my daughter, Beth, for believing her mother could complete the project with some long-distance cheerleading; and my parents who taught me to always believe in myself and reach for the stars, even when those stars were not what was expected. Most of all to my dearest friend and mentor, Jody, for believing that even I can teach and conduct action research.

Table of Contents

INTRODUCTION

"Do I always have to cover for teachers' planning time? How am I going to order new books when I am teaching throughout the day? If I am covering for planning time, when am I going to collaborate with the teachers? Will a flexible schedule affect student achievement? How can I be certain that I am truly helping students succeed?"

School library media specialists are asking themselves these and many other questions on a daily basis. The literature in the library field is filled with research to address the flexible scheduling issue and other library-related situations.

These articles oftentimes discuss the issues theoretically and are not focused on individual circumstances. Library media specialists need to understand this theory and then apply it to their own professional situations through the practice of action research. The purpose of this book is to give library media specialists the skills they need to use action research for reflective problem solving in their schools.

The ability to develop and conduct action research is a necessary skill for the library media specialist. The school library media specialist, an integral part of the instructional leadership team, must have knowledge of and skill in conducting action research. The school library media specialist has not only the total school picture, but also the classroom orientation and vision for developing the action research process. The results obtained through action research are essential for school improvement, accountability, and student achievement.

Accountability for the library media specialist is synonymous with student achievement. *Information Power: Building Partnerships for Learning* describes the role of the library media specialist as encompassing three areas: instruction, information access, and program administration. Learning the steps needed to conduct action research will give the library media specialist the skills she needs to improve her program. She will reflect upon her entire program and determine what needs to be changed or adapted to assist students in becoming lifelong learners. In her instructional leadership role, she will be prepared to work with her administrators and staff to use reflective problem solving for school improvement.

We have worked in school libraries as library media specialists with all grade levels and with students of various ethnicities, backgrounds, and beliefs. We have worked at the building, district, and university levels. Our collective experiences have shown us that reflective problem solving is a must for the leadership role of the school library media specialist.

Recently, we found ourselves co-teaching a class of budding library media specialists how to conduct their own action research. We found a passable general education action research text. Material pertinent to school libraries needed to be developed, outside readings researched and assigned, and we soon realized there was a definite lack of resources available for school library media specialists in the area of action research.

Having long understood that in education, "Where there is need, fill it," we undertook the process of developing and revising our syllabus and materials with enthusiasm. We were very excited when we found a clearer way to explain the action research process for library media specialists to our students. At first, we were greeted with puzzled student reactions during our weekly meetings. How could we possibly be thrilled with any kind of research? As processes and purposes were clarified and living library examples were shared, our students came to realize the fundamental reasons for conducting action research. Library examples made the process clearer since those applications related to the students' professional surroundings.

Educators have become more aware of the value of action research during the past decade and as we were developing our research, we realized that many practicing library media specialists will need to learn or refresh their skills in this area. There is a need for a simple guide and explanation of how to use action research for reflective problem solving. This book explains the steps of action research with examples from the daily life of library media specialists. Using this context will provide the practitioner with a resource for reflective problem solving in her own school library media center. Although this book is designed specifically for improvement of practices connected with school libraries, the applications and implications can be interpreted into other areas of the school and community.

We are excited about the possibilities of providing this tool for individuals or school teams as they design school improvement efforts. The text can be used for staff development exercises within districts and also for classroom teachers working collaboratively with others.

The book presents a step-by-step process for conducting action research in a school library, and an outline of the process necessary to complete a valid and reliable project. The book contains a scenario of an action research project conducted at the middle school level. We will introduce Megan, the school library media specialist at Mountain Ridge Middle School. This scenario will provide examples of each step in the action research process. Instructional charts, survey samples, and learning aids that Megan developed are included.

Chapter 1 defines action research and illustrates the differences between action research and traditional research. In Chapter 2, tips are given on how to select a topic and examine professional resources through a literature review. Chapter 3 explores the need for assessing the environment, along with the library and school situation prior to beginning a project. The assessment includes goals, languages, cultural symbols, diversity, population, staff information, and economic factors. Developing the problem statement and creating research questions are addressed in Chapter 4. Chapter 5 discusses the tools and methods for collecting data. Chapter 6 considers the elements necessary to produce a valid and reliable project. Chapter 7 shows how to analyze and interpret data, including tips on coding the data. Action research never ends; Chapter 8 illustrates the spiral effect and assessment of the project's results. Chapter 9 offers tips on sharing findings with others in the library and educational arena.

Following Chapter 9 we have included additional information which will be of benefit to library media specialists. Appendix 1 includes professional journals willing to accept educational articles for publication. Appendix 2 provides a complete action research study conducted at an elementary school. Appendix 3 is an annotated list of helpful action research Web sites. Appendix 4 offers an annotated list of recommended resources. We have included a glossary of terms which will be helpful in understanding the topic of action research. An index is provided to assist in the location of specific subjects.

Novices in the action research field will profit from reading this text from cover to cover. Practitioners will find the information they need by using the index and table of contents. This book offers assistance to beginners in the field of action research and to professionals who need review in the action research arena.

A Note Concerning Gender

Libraries are not a sexist environment, but for ease of reading and understanding, the authors have chosen to use the terms "she" and "her" to refer to school library media specialists rather than confuse the audience. We have used the terms solely out of convenience, and there is no intention to exclude the male gender from the field of study. Men have always worked side-by-side with women in our libraries and we celebrate that fact.

A Note on Terminology

Throughout the United States and the world, many different terms are used to describe the person who runs the school library program. They are: library media specialist, librarian, school librarian, library information specialist, teacher librarian, information specialist, library teacher, and a variety of others. We have elected to use the term "library media specialist" to describe the professionals holding this position.

1

Stepping Into Action

The Why of Action Research

- A library media specialist in an elementary school has the students coming in each day on a fixed schedule so that the classroom teachers will be able to have planning time.
- A library media specialist in a middle school of 1200 students has very little paraprofessional assistance in the library.
- A high school library media specialist has 3600 students and her role is to develop a collaborative program based on *Information Power: Building Partnerships for Learning*, published by the American Association of School Librarians and the Association for Educational Communications and Technology.

The examples above describe situations which are common in library media centers today. Many days we walk into the library facing issues like those described above or move from task to task without having time to stop and reflect upon the important role we play in the academic achievement of the students in our schools and in the professional development of the teachers in our buildings. Our schedule rarely allows us time for reflective thinking or planning. Yet, without reflective thinking and planning, the hamster wheel we are on can last for days, weeks, and months. We begin each year with high expectations of accomplishing many goals, but reality sets in as we work day by day just to keep our heads above water. This situation is why, as library media specialists, we must allow time for assessing our professional situations to determine where we are going and why. We must reflect; through reflection we determine the methods we will use to develop and improve our programs.

Reflective practice moves us forward. It precipitates professional growth and allows us to be sure that our day-to-day activities are actually promoting student achievement reflected in a plan for accomplishing the goals of our school and our program. As library media specialists, we should be leaders in our school, meshing our program with the mission, vision, and goals of the entire school. As library media specialists, we work collaboratively with the classroom teachers to insure that our students are able to find, access, evaluate, analyze, synthesize, and create information. Our role is to assure that students and staff members in our schools have command of the information literacy skills as personal resources that they are able to use as they become lifelong learners. We promote, increase, and enhance student achievement. The school library has been described as the "hub or heart of the school" in the literature for many years. In order to make a library the hub of the school, school library media specialists must provide leadership in reflective practice. As members of the school's instructional team, the library media specialist is the "go to" person to implement this reflective practice.

School Improvement and Accountability

Educationally, the mechanism that drives reflective planning is the need for accountability, school improvement, and student achievement. These three terms are known in educational circles by various names and are assessed in various manners. Regardless of the term used, each school achieves improvement, accountability, and success for all students by determining its mission, vision, goals, and methods that the staff will use to accomplish these goals. Effective planning involves all of the stakeholders: administrators, staff, parents, members of the community, and students. The library media specialist must provide leadership in assisting the principal and staff with the necessary planning and reflection.

The What of Action Research

The act of reflective planning is action research. Farmer in *How to Conduct Action Research: A Guide for Library Media Specialists* describes action research as a process analyzing our own situations and professional practices in order to improve methodologies. Farmer states that the action research process requires reflecting, planning, and action. These three component parts are necessary for positive change to occur.

The library media specialist can use action research to improve her instruction, the information access she provides for the students, and the necessary components of managing the school library program. On a grander scale, the library media specialist can collaborate with the administration and staff to conduct action research promoting student achievement on a school-wide basis. Whether it is a library or classroom related problem, or a situation which affects the larger school community, the library media specialist provides the leadership necessary to change and improve the program. Action research is the vehicle the library media specialist uses to analyze a situation and determine what needs to be done to address the issue.

Geoffrey Mills in the 2nd edition of *Action Research: A Guide for the Teacher Researcher* defines action research as:

Any systematic inquiry conducted by teacher researchers, principals, school counselors, or other stakeholders in the teaching/learning environment to gather information about how their particular schools operate, how they teach, and how well their students learn. This information is gathered with the goals of gaining insight, developing reflective practice, effecting positive changes in school environment (and on educational practices in general), and improving students outcomes and the lives of those involved. (5)

Reflective Practice

Commonly referred to as the father of action research, Kurt Lewin (1890-1947) in his article "Action Research and Minority Problems" indicates traditional research conducted seeking global truths and solutions did not necessarily help the individual practitioner at the local level. Solutions from established research provide a valid and reliable answer but might not help the practitioner with individual circumstances. Action research for improvement must be conducted in a specific arena. A key component of this research is reflective practice. Practitioners constantly analyze their own library media centers and classrooms reflecting on what needs to be changed or implemented to promote student achievement. This reflection generates kernels of ideas which help the library media specialist say, "What if I changed this procedure, process, or instructional practice? Would it subsequently increase the student learning occurring through the library media center?" Or the reflection might take the form of a "Why" question. "Why are the students having problems learning the information literacy standards? What can I change or implement to increase their knowledge and learning?" This reflection should then lead to concrete actions for program improvement and student achievement. This is reflective practice: analyzing a problem and making a commitment to improve one's practice by following a series of steps. Reflective practice is the basis of action research.

Action Research Versus Traditional Research

It is important to understand the difference between action research and the traditional form of research. One of the most recent examples of traditional research in our field is the work of Keith Curry Lance in his studies concerning the relationship between the school library program and student achievement. In his studies, Lance has developed a hypothesis, accounted for variables, is able to predict future outcomes based upon the data he has collected, and has identified the qualities necessary for powerful library media programs. He has replicated his work in a variety of school districts and states with each example producing similar results. This process is a form of traditional research. The researcher accounts for specific criteria and is able to make general statements concerning that research. It is then applicable to more than one situation.

Action research is about a definite time and a specific place. It is about a professional situation accounting for the learning community's needs for improvement in certain areas. Although the solutions developed at a school work for their specific situation, those solutions may not work for any other school or educational setting. Action research includes reflective practice for improvement within the school community. The following are examples of traditional and action research.

Traditional Research

A school library media specialist is required to produce a master's level thesis in order to graduate from a library program. She decides that she would like to determine if there is any relationship between the use of an automated reading assessment program such as Accelerated Reader or Reading Counts and the improvement of the students' reading ability. She will need to define her parameters, determine her control group, her experimental group, the random sample she will take, and the statistical analysis program she will use to interpret this data. When she has completed this study, she will publish her findings in various academic journals.

Action Research

A library media specialist is hired to replace a librarian who has been at an elementary school for 12 years. During the previous 12 years, the school librarian has had a fixed library schedule and has been involved in the specials' rotation, which allows the classroom teachers to have common planning time. The new library media specialist realizes that she must have access to the classroom teachers during their planning time so that they can collaborate on activities that will increase the academic achievement of the students. That will be impossible with this fixed schedule as part of the specials' rotation. She decides to begin collecting data on how a change in the library schedule at her school can occur and what benefits that change will have for her staff and students.

Figure 1.1 below illustrates the differences between traditional and action research.

Figure 1.1 Traditional Versus Action Research. Adapted from Mills and Schmuck.

Traditional Research	Action Research
Usually conducted at the university or state level by professors, graduate students, or professional researchers. Researchers are often removed from the actual research sites.	Conducted at your own school site utilizing your expertise and that of your principal and your staff.
Accounts for specific variables with control groups and experimental groups. The data collection is very objective.	Reflection on the parameters at your school using the information about your students.
Uses quantitative methods to collect data that provides a statistical significance in a cause and effect relationship between variables. Uses very little qualitative data.	Uses quantitative and qualitative data to describe the school environment and to determine a course of action for improvement.
Uses results to publish conclusions to be used as generalities in the field.	Uses results to implement programs that will effect positive change for school improvement that can be shared with colleagues through publications.

Advantages and Disadvantages of Action Research

Action research is a reflective means of problem solving. Its purpose is to analyze a situation and determine if the situation can be improved in any manner. Looking at the researcher's personal school surroundings, the library media specialist can determine what process needs to be examined. Since this research is an area which affects the library media specialist's work, there will be immediate buy-in as to the process. The researcher does not need to confine the areas to be examined to the library itself, but can and should also be the catalyst to reflecting on problems and questions affecting the entire school community. This personalization of problem solving is one advantage of action research. It is accomplished at the local level involving the stakeholders who want to make their school more productive for student achievement. The local touch and community investment are present. Action research can be conducted without a group of researchers outside of the school building being involved. It is a personal solution to problems in the school.

The data collection for these projects is also easier to accomplish since the data collected directly involve the students, staff, and school community at the local level. Some projects rely upon data in the library, and some projects will require comparison data from a neighboring or similar school. In either of these circumstances, the researcher will have less data to collect and analyze since the research is on a smaller scale than a traditional research project conducted at the university or national level.

One disadvantage of action research is that even though the researcher has access to the data, collecting it does take time. Data instruments need to be developed, and the collected results need to be analyzed. Fitting this additional process into an already busy day is sometimes challenging.

When a university professor conducts research in the field of education, this process lends credence to the outcomes of the project. This university involvement promotes the objectivity of the research. Consumers of the research expect the study to be valid and reliable since the research has been conducted in the academic arena. When action research is conducted at the school level, these two factors can be questioned since the situations being examined are local and personal. The library media specialist must be circumspect in accounting for the validity and reliability of data collection and interpretation. Both reliability and validity must be accounted for so that the practitioner is assured that the change or implementation does support improvement in professional practice.

Traditional research and action research use both quantitative data and qualitative data. Quantitative data is numbers data. This type of data allows the researcher to collect answers to questions through counting like answers or responses. Qualitative data results from open-ended questions. Qualitative data requires time to analyze the respondents' answers as they are providing more information than a "yes" or "no" response. Action researchers are able to use qualitative data effectively since their projects are conducted on a smaller scale. See Figure 1.2 for the advantages and disadvantages of action research.

Figure 1.2 Advantages and Disadvantages of Action Research.

Advantages	Disadvantages
Problem solving at the local level.	Absence of university backing.
Ease of data collection.	Reliability and validity could be concerns.
Support of participants.	Organizing time to accomplish the reflective planning.

Chapter One: Stepping Into Action Research

The Action Research Spiral

One beauty of action research is that it is the beginning of a continual process of improvement in professional practice. The practitioner reflects on an area that needs to be improved. The practitioner then determines the focus, collects data, analyzes the data, outlines a plan of action, implements the plan, and evaluates the results of the plan. As the practitioner reflects on the results, the spiral begins again, leading to additional data collection, analysis of data, an additional plan of action, another implementation of the plan, and evaluation of results. This process is the action research cycle.

There are many visual representations of the process of action research. Mills in the 2nd edition of his work *Action Research: A Guide for the Teacher Researcher*, Schmuck in *Practical Action Research for Change*, and Johnson in *A Short Guide to Action Research* provide various examples of these visual representations. These examples contain three basic steps: Reflect, analyze, and implement. This is action research. Action research can be thought of as a spiral (Figure 1.3), a simple line drawing with the preceding three areas. The spiral does not end since the results of the action need to be reflected upon and then the process begins again. Using this continuous spiral of action research, the library media specialist will be assured of continuous program improvement for the academic achievement of her students.

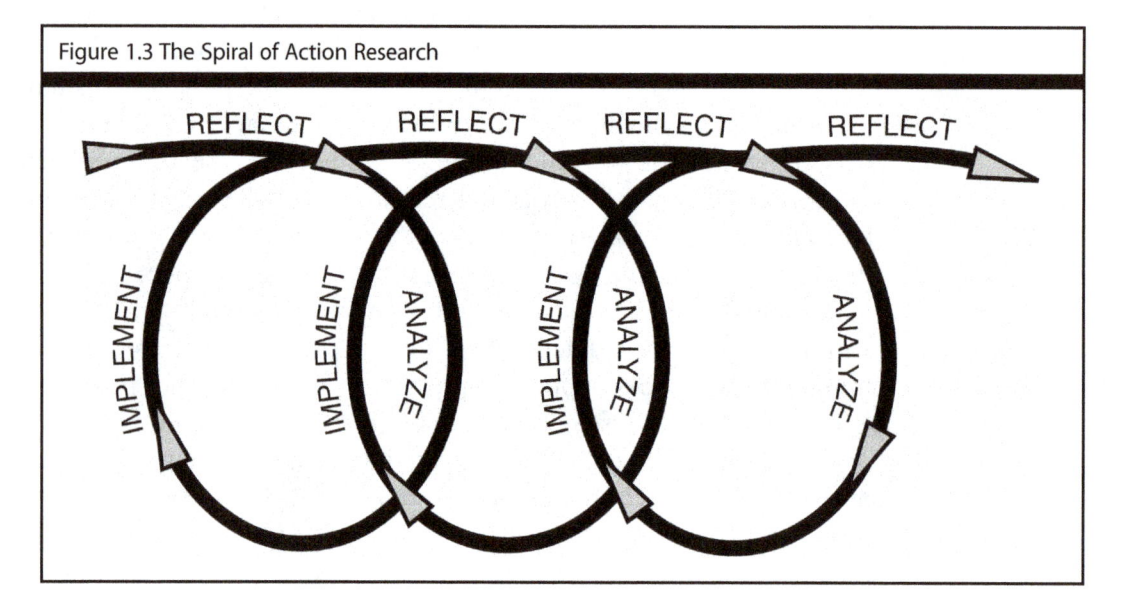

Figure 1.3 The Spiral of Action Research

Schmuck illustrates two different versions of action research. Both methods show the continuous spiraling effect of research. The difference is the point of origin. The researcher may decide to implement a new program or try a new practice. The researcher will implement the program and then collect and analyze the data to determine if the new program is stimulating increased student achievement. Schmuck describes this as Proactive Action Research. The researcher may decide to examine an existing practice. The researcher begins by reflecting on the existing practice, by collecting the data, analyzing the data, and then implementing a plan of action. Schmuck identifies this method as Responsive Action Research. The library media specialist must decide which of the two methods she will use as she plans her project.

Action Research Scenario

Action research should be real. To help understand the process, we have developed a scenario which will be used in the upcoming chapters. The scenario will allow readers to experience an actual situation as we examine the component parts of a successful action research project.

> **Action Research Scenario**
>
> Megan Jones was recently hired as the library media specialist at Mountain Ridge Middle School. Prior to her employment, classes were scheduled into the library on a fixed rotation. The sixth grade classes had an assigned check-out slot each week and had library skills presented to them in an isolated setting. The seventh and eighth grade classes were also assigned to weekly checkouts with research units on a rotating basis. Megan had learned the advantages of a flexible schedule in her library school coursework and believed a flexible schedule was the best means to help students gain the skills necessary to be lifelong learners. She also knew she should reflect upon the existing situation before she implemented any radical changes. Megan decided to continue with this schedule until she could find out if it was workable for her situation or not.

Using this scenario as a basis, we will begin to look at the components necessary for action research. Megan will need to refine her topic, develop a problem statement, review the literature, analyze the environment, formulate a research question, create an action plan, collect data, assess the process, and make any needed plans for the future.

Chapter Summary

In Chapter 1 we have looked at why it is important for educational professionals to engage in action research. We have seen that action research is a means of accomplishing school improvement, student achievement, and accountability. Action research is a reflective professional practice. This research differs from traditional research as it is conducted at the school level examining problems pertinent to specific professional situations. The advantages of action research include problem solving at the local level, ease of data collection, and support of the participants. The disadvantages are the absence of the university backing, concerns about reliability and validity, and finding the time to accomplish the data collection and interpretation. Action research is a continuous spiral of school improvement including the stages of reflecting, analyzing, and implementing.

2
Exploring the Topic

Booth, Colomb, and Williams in *The Craft of Research* state that most research of any merit begins with an "intellectual itch that only one person feels the need to scratch" (35). One of these intellectual itches can provide the content of action research. As the library media specialist is reflecting on her current program and how she can improve it, she may decide to explore one of these "intellectual itches." We have seen that action research involves a school situation which needs to be examined to determine if a change would help increase student achievement. Conducting this research will be another item to fit into an already busy schedule, so the researcher needs to be certain that the area of focus relates to student learning.

Selecting the Topic

There are various ways of determining topics for action research. Sagor in *Guiding School Improvement with Action Research,* Farmer, and Mills present detailed explanations about this process. The researcher should be aware of the following items when determining a topic for research.

- All action research should revolve around student achievement or improvement of the staff as professionals. This focus is the purpose of education and should be the focus of any problem-solving and reflective practice.

- The research area should be within the researcher's scope of authority. The purpose of action research is to implement positive change. If the researcher does not have any authority over the area being researched, then the process is for naught.

The topic selected should be one that the library media specialist has an interest in or is passionate about scrutinizing. It can also be an area which the researcher realizes is a problem that needs to be evaluated. The interest must be there, or it will be difficult to maintain the enthusiasm while participating in the action research cycle.

When exploring ideas to be developed into action research projects, the action researcher must decide whether she will be examining a library project dealing with the library program only or whether the project will be a school-wide effort involving the entire school or the school community. Action research is quickly becoming a reality in many educational settings and the library media specialist should take a leadership role in any projects which will increase student achievement in the school community.

The library media specialist may have a clear idea of what area or problem needs to be tackled through action research. Sometimes, however, there are many areas which need attention or there is not a clear indication of what the problem really is. In order to determine the parameters of the problem, the researcher may spend a few days or weeks writing in a journal. To use a professional journal effectively, the researcher should write in the journal each day for five to ten minutes. This activity should be a simple reflection about what has occurred in the library during the day. It can also include any interactions the action researcher has with staff members when they are discussing school problems. The library media specialist should note any circumstances which affect student learning and flag these items to be analyzed at a later time. After a week or so, the library media specialist should re-read her entries and see if she can determine any patterns which have developed. If the researcher notices that there is a bottleneck of students in the library during the lunch hour and the library is used more as a recreational area, maybe the action research should revolve around the use of the library during lunch periods. If the school library media specialist notices through the entries in her journal that many of the staff members are concerned about access to the library because of the schedule, then the action research might revolve around the library schedule. If the staff expresses concerns about the implementation of the new math program in the school, then the researcher should explore the possibility of a collaborative action research project involving the math teachers and other staff members the math program implementation will affect.

Keeping a journal can be viewed as difficult by some because it is adding another job to accomplish in a full schedule. Committing to keeping a journal a few minutes each day will help the library media specialist discover recurring patterns that she might not have known were present. Journaling will assist the researcher in identifying an area which needs reflective problem solving.

Collaborative brainstorming is another way the library media specialist can hone in on areas needing to be improved through action research. This brainstorming can be accomplished in a variety of ways. One way is for the researcher to organize a meeting with interested staff members and have a dialogue based on general questions affecting the school. These open-ended questions should focus on student achievement or staff improvement. If one group of students scored significantly lower on an assessment than was expected, then

10 Action Research: A Guide for Library Media Specialists

the question could be asked, "Why did the fifth graders score lower on their reading assessment than the fourth graders?" "Did the environmental surroundings during the testing period affect the outcomes of the test?" If the staff morale is low, one open-ended question could address that issue. "Why is staff morale different this year than it was last year?" "What can we do about it?" "How is staff morale affecting student achievement?"

Maybe the problem-solving focus is more library related. If it is, then the action researcher can host a similar brainstorming session with other library media specialists either in person or through electronic means. E-lists are informative ways to brainstorm ideas. They are a means of electronic reflective thinking. If the library media specialist realizes that her program needs to be re-energized, then a good brainstorming question might be: "How can I re-infuse energy into my program?" Whether through posting to an e-list or through a comfortable meeting with peers or fellow staff members, open-ended questions can stimulate reflective thinking which will help determine what needs to be explored further to improve student achievement.

Sagor suggests a *reflective interview* as a means of determining a topic to be explored through action research. He encourages the researcher to choose a partner who is a good listener and spend 20 minutes with that partner explaining the area of concern to that person. The listener does not make any suggestions, share any opinions, or make any judgments on the topic. The listener is only allowed to ask clarifying questions. At the end of the 20 minutes, the researcher should be able to determine if this problem is a topic that is worth the time to explore through action research. If the topic fizzles out during the discussion, then it probably will not be a good action research topic. The researcher may be able to solve the problem through this discussion by thinking of a less formal solution than participating in action research.

Megan's Process of Topic Selection

Megan used a combination of all of the previous methods to determine how she should proceed with her reflective problem solving. She employed a basic management principle which encourages new managers to refrain from implementing any drastic changes for the first few weeks on the job. Megan worked within the existing fixed schedule for the first few weeks of school so that she could determine the good and the bad points of the schedule. When Megan realized how limiting the schedule was, she approached the principal to discuss the possibility of implementing a flexible schedule as soon as possible.

Soon after she was hired, Megan participated in a reflective interview with the former librarian who had retired from Mountain Ridge. Megan decided that having the retired librarian listen to how she perceived the schedule in relation to student achievement would assist her in pinpointing the validity of trying to implement a different schedule. Megan wanted to learn her predecessor's reason for using a fixed schedule and the impact the schedule had on student achievement.

Megan also participated in a brainstorming session with her peers at the first library meeting. This brainstorming session helped Megan understand that she needed to address the library schedule through an action research project.

Due to discussions of *best practices* in her library classes and the emphasis on flexible scheduling, Megan was certain that she wanted to change from a fixed schedule to a flexible schedule. She again approached her principal to explain how she would conduct action research to determine if a flexible schedule would help increase student achievement.

Joyce, in her article "Fostering Reading Through Intrinsic Motivation: An Action Research Study," and Farmer offer excellent lists of topics that are appropriate to explore through action research. The following is a list of other possible library-related questions that might be reflected upon.

- Should we adopt a new library automation system?
- What computer platform should be used: Macintosh or PC?
- Which informational databases will best increase student achievement?
- How should I increase my collaboration with the classroom teachers?
- Is there a relationship between sustained silent reading and student achievement?
- Do products such as Accelerated Reader and Reading Counts support student achievement?
- How can the library program increase student achievement?
- How effective is information literacy instruction?
- Should the library implement flexible or fixed scheduling?
- Can the school library media specialist effectively fulfill the role of library media specialist and technology specialist?
- Is there sufficient staffing in the library to support instruction of information literacy standards and student achievement?

School library media specialists, in their leadership role, should be aware of the areas of school improvement that can be examined through action research. The following list identifies possible school-related topics or questions for study.

- When a high percentage of second language students make up a student body, should only one language be used for instruction?
- Should computer labs be replaced with wireless technology?
- Are the needs of the special population students being met? (gifted and talented, special education, second language learners)
- How many computers should be in each classroom to increase student achievement?
- How does student attitude throughout the school affect student learning?
- Does a full-day kindergarten increase student achievement?

The above examples illustrate the types of problems that may be effectively analyzed through action research. The library media specialist and staff through collaborative brainstorming, reflective interviews, and journaling can determine when and how to use action research in their school setting as a means of problem solving for the increase of student learning.

Reviewing the Literature

Library media specialists are in the business of information literacy. A basic focus through the information literacy standards is to help students and others find information and organize that information. Library media specialists know the basics of reviewing the literature and organizing the information found during the review. Focusing on the topic for action research, the library media specialist needs to search the existing professional literature to find what others have already written about the topic. Maybe other library media specialists have already found solutions for similar problems and the action researcher will be able to adapt this research to her own situation. This search allows the researcher to frame the topic in a theoretical context. As the researcher reviews these sources, she examines what other professionals have already determined about the topic and can see how this information might be used in her professional surroundings.

As library media specialists have conducted research in other surroundings, they have determined what methods work best for them. Maybe the individual works best with reviewing sources and then taking notes on index cards. Possibly the researcher organizes notes through the use of a laptop, PDA, tablet, or pocket PC. Perhaps the researcher reads with a highlighter in her hand marking the points that will be relevant to the topic. The process of taking notes does not matter. What does matter is that as the researcher reviews professional sources, she needs to have a method that works well and allows her to organize the important facts from the articles being reviewed. Regardless of the system the researcher uses, it should be flexible enough to organize all of the information about certain aspects of the topic into identified groupings. Using index cards allows this flexibility, but the researcher can also word process notes and then organize them by topic either through the "sort" function or printing out the notes and then organizing them in stacks according to designated subtopics. If the library media specialist is transcribing notes by hand, it is best to use only one side of the paper to allow for this flexibility of organization.

Not so many years ago, it was very difficult to find information on one's topic. That is not the problem today, and the wealth of information at our fingertips is many times too much for us to sift through and synthesize. The following steps will assist the researcher in retrieving the information which will be valuable in searching the professional sources.

> *Find a library:* The researcher needs to find a good academic library to use to begin a search. Academic libraries have a wide variety of sources available for use by students and staff. If the action researcher is not associated with an academic library, then she must determine what arrangements she can make to have access to the library's print and electronic sources. Many times having a public library card will also allow the action researcher to have access to the sources at the local academic library. If an academic library is not available in the area, then the library media specialist should work with the local public library. Public libraries will not have the specialized sources which the academic library will have, but the general sources will be a starting place for the research. If the school district has a professional library, many times the researcher will find useful sources in that collection.
>
> *Find a librarian:* Most libraries have staff members who are trained in the reference area. Work with this person, regardless of whether they are at the school, the district, an academic library, or a public library. The reference librarian will assist the researcher in finding the sources that are needed. Even though as library media specialists, we know the basic sources, we

do not know what sources are available at a specific institution. That is the beauty of working with the librarian. She knows the sources at her library and will help the researcher unlock the doors to the needed information.

Explore print sources: With the explosion of the Internet, we sometimes forget that there is still a wealth of information available in print format. Access the online catalog to see what books, government documents, monographs, or periodicals are at the library. Either review these on the spot or check them out for later perusal.

Explore electronic sources: Many libraries subscribe to online databases. The researcher should explore these and find out which one(s) are applicable to her topic. There are databases which are devoted to library literature and the library media specialist can begin her exploration by accessing these sources. H.W. Wilson provides an index and full text for a variety of library literature through the *Library Literature and Information Science Full Text*. This source indexes English and foreign-language periodicals, including state publications, conference proceedings, books, and library school theses. The *Librarians Information Online Network* (LION) is also useful to the researcher. This source sponsored by EBSCO provides access to 30 library journals including *Electronic School* and *School Libraries Worldwide*. The library media specialist should also access the ALA Web site where she will have access to the ALA publications including *School Library Media Research* and *School Library Journal*. In addition, the Web sites of specific library periodicals, such as *Teacher Librarian* and *Library Media Connection* are available. These publications have a wealth of information that the library media specialist can access through the search function on the Web sites. For general education articles, a useful source is the *ERIC* (Educational Resources Information Center) database. This database contains journals and research reports on many subjects in the educational field. *ERIC* is accessible through print, microfiche or online. By using the online version of *ERIC*, the researcher will be able to peruse her topic or similar examples located at the same Web site. *ERIC* provides abstracts to various articles, but there may be a fee to retrieve the entire text. Other databases such as *EBSCO Host*, *ProQuest*, and *OCLC FirstSearch* are also available and can be accessed either at the library or through a home computer using specific library passwords obtained by using one's library card. Conducting a search on the Internet using search engines such as Google, Yahoo, Dog Pile, or AltaVista will also provide the researcher with relevant information and sources. Since these search engines include sources from all realms of information, each source must be scrutinized for its accuracy and validity.

Find the interlibrary loan department (ILL): Most libraries have an ILL department. The staff in this department will order many books or resources which are not available on site. When using ILL the action researcher will need to allow for the time it will take to have the materials sent to the library. Another item to note is that the researcher may only keep the materials for a certain amount of time. Both of these time factors need to be considered when requesting materials through ILL.

Read abstracts: With the plethora of sources available, the researcher needs to be aware of the useful information found in the source's abstract. The abstract is a short summary of the actual article or monograph, usually 150-200 words long. Reading this information will help the action researcher determine if she needs to retrieve the full source.

Prepare a graphic organizer: The number of sources the library media specialist finds in the literature search will depend on the nature of the topic. The field of library literature is extensive, and if the researcher is exploring the effects of collaboration with the classroom teacher or the implementation of information literacy standards in the school setting, she is likely to find myriad sources. All of the sources will not be exactly what the researcher is looking for but may be helpful. The library media specialist needs a means to see at a glance which title addresses the concept she is exploring. Mills suggests that the action researcher prepare a Literature Matrix to keep track of the variables which are addressed in the sources that have been examined. Preparing a graphic organizer similar to the one he suggests gives a quick visual representation of the contents of the articles. This organizer should include the author, title, copyright date, and focus of the article similar to Figure 2.1.

As the library media specialist is conducting her literature review, she must be aware of the source of the articles she reads. Some articles may contain only one person's opinion and may be a subjective review of that person's experience. The action researcher needs to scrutinize these articles to determine if the author conducted research using a research process or if it is a subjective relating of information. During the literature review, the library media specialist may find that her topic has already been researched and the conclusions reached will answer her question. Analyzing these sources in this manner will assist the researcher in planning the types of data she will want to collect while conducting her research.

Figure 2.1 Literature Review Graphic Organizer, Adapted from Mills (40).

Literature Review Graphic Organizer

Author	Title	Year	Focus

The following are tips for conducting a review of the literature.

1. Review and personalize your method of taking notes
2. Find a library.
3. Find a librarian.
4. Explore print sources.
5. Explore electronic sources.
6. Locate the interlibrary loan department.
7. Read the abstracts.
8. Prepare a graphic organizer visually depicting the content of the sources.
9. Evaluate the sources.

Megan's Literature Review

Figure 2.2 is a portion of the graphic organizer which Megan designed. The organizer provided her with a visual representation of the articles she found during her review of the professional literature.

Figure 2.2 Megan's Literature Review Graphic Organizer

Literature Review Graphic Organizer

Author	Title	Year	Focus			
			Flexible scheduling	Fixed scheduling	Student acheivement	Collaboration
Orlich, K. B.	Timing is Everything	1989	*		*	*
Orlich, K. B.	Making Flexible Access & Flexible Scheduling Work Today	2001	*		*	
Lance, K.	The Impact of School Library Media Centers on Academic Achievement	1994	*	*	*	*
Lance, K.	The Second Colorado Study	2000	*	*	*	*
Van Deusen, J.	The Effects of Fixed Versus Flexible Scheduling on Curriculum Involvement and Skills Integration in School Library Media Programs	1993	*	*	*	*
Bernstein, A.	Flexible Schedules Quality Learning Time	1997	*	*	*	
Rogers, P.	The Positive Qualities of a Fixed Schedule	1992		*		

16 Action Research: A Guide for Library Media Specialists

Chapter Summary

In Chapter 2 we explored how to narrow the topic of an action research question. Sometimes the need for improvement is readily apparent. If the researcher is having trouble determining the parameters of the topic, she may brainstorm with colleagues or keep a journal noting patterns calling for improvement. After the researcher has selected the topic, she should review the professional literature in order to determine what has been previously written concerning her topic. The library media specialist should find a library, a librarian, explore print and electronic resources, request materials through interlibrary loan, determine the content of the materials, prepare a graphic organizer to depict the results of her literature search, and evaluate the sources she located.

3

Assessing the Environment

After completing the literature review, it is now time to look at the action research environment. The setting will give the action researcher a sound understanding of the influences which might affect the project. The researcher must be aware of the existing factors which could alter the results of the action research project. Three areas need to be analyzed: the community, the school itself, and the library.

The Community

There are various factors to consider when analyzing the community that surrounds the school. The researcher should determine which of these factors could have a bearing on the project and explore these areas to gain the answers to the following questions:

Ethnicity:
- What is the predominant language spoken in the homes?
- What is the cultural make-up of the people living in the area?
- Do the children speak one language at home and another at school?
- Do the parents speak English?

Family Structure:
- Does the family consist of a father as breadwinner and the mother who is a homemaker?
- Do both of the parents work outside the home?
- Are there many single-parent homes?
- Do the children split their time between two households?

- Does the family include an extended family of grandmother, grandfather, aunt, or uncle?
- How many families are considered large (three or more children)?

Religious Values:
- Do members of the community all support one religion?
- Is there a predominance of religious practices that take place in the community?
- Are there religions with divergent viewpoints competing for members in the community?

Economics:
- Is the community made up of mainly blue-collar workers?
- Is the community made up of workers in the professional area?
- Are there businesses or industries in the community that have an impact on the school?
- What is the academic level of the parents?
- Do the parents have high school diplomas?
- Are the parents educated to the BA/BS, MA, or Ph.D. level?

Community Attitude Towards the School:
- Is the school a building that is used only for educating students during the day?
- Is the school the center of the community being used for church, sports events, and community gatherings?

Other Resources:
- Is there a public library that is a valuable part of the community?
- Are there businesses that could provide partnerships with the school for specific projects?
- Are there other entities that would be interested in school/community partnerships?

These are sample questions the researcher can use while examining the community. During this reflection, the researcher should explore all areas that will give a thorough background for the research project. The answers to the questions will provide the library media specialist with a context that will surround this inquiry and assist with determining the influences affecting the outcomes of the project. The answers to these questions may show the action researcher areas where further data may need to be collected. The following example illustrates how the library media specialist discovered specific community factors which would influence her action research project.

> ## Community Influence
>
> Beth was concerned about how to communicate with the students in her school since many of them came from Spanish-speaking families. She determined that she needed to know the extent of the population in her area that fit this profile. She looked at her community and found that 49% of the 800 students coming to her school came from families where Spanish was spoken as the primary language in the home. She also determined that poverty was a factor as 77% of the students received assistance through federal funds providing free and reduced lunches. The essence of Beth's research was to discover whether she should speak Spanish to the students when she interacted with them or whether it would be better to immerse them in English. She needed to determine which course of action would best increase student achievement. The community information she gathered provided one piece of the puzzle she was trying to solve.

Many entities exist where researchers can gain assistance in understanding the community. The local visitors' bureau, chamber of commerce, and real estate agents will be able to give the researcher a good sense of the make-up of the community. If the researcher has access to the Web, much of this information can be found by exploring Web sites. City Web sites list information from the local chamber of commerce and the visitors' bureau. Some agencies have a section that provides information for new residents. All list phone numbers that will guide the researcher to departments that will provide needed information. The researcher should also access state and federal Web sites to find additional information about her local community.

The researcher should check the school district public information office. The school district's annual report has pertinent data that the researcher may use for discovering background information about the community. If more data is needed, the researcher should contact the school district public information officer and this person can provide additional facts and figures.

The School

The researcher should next turn her attention to gathering information about the school. As a staff member, the library media specialist will already have some of the pertinent information. Now is the time to analyze more deeply the school situation and the essence of the school. Each year the school is involved in the process of planning for improvement to enhance student achievement. Specific goals are established, and the staff uses these goals to focus student learning. The library media specialist should be aware of the goals and how they fit into the mission statement and vision of the school. She should also be very honest about analyzing the staff's response to these goals and direction. When conducting action research, the researcher will obtain more accurate results if there is a good understanding of the atmosphere of the school, including the staff's support for the administration and the school's vision. Vision statements and goals can be either words on a piece of paper or they can be a driving force that unites the faculty.

Finding answers to the following questions will assist the researcher in gathering this information.

Principal:
- What is the principal's leadership style?
- Does the principal lead informally or formally?
- Does the principal make decisions and then inform the staff?
- Does the principal work collaboratively with the staff?
- Who are the members of the principal's administrative team?

Staff:
- Is the staff willing to follow the principal's lead?
- Is the staff a cohesive group willing to support each other?
- Are there cliques either by grade level, content areas, or longevity in the building that influence ownership or the way decisions are made?
- Are the teachers new to the profession or are they seasoned veterans?
- How large is the staff?
- Is the staff liberal or conservative?

Atmosphere:
- Is the school atmosphere cooperative or filled with tension?
- Do visitors to the school feel energy and enthusiasm?
- Do community members and visitors feel welcome?
- Does the staff feel that the school is a good place to work?

Students:
- What is the student enrollment?
- How do the students feel about the school?
- Do the students see the school as a place they want to be?
- Do they feel they are valued?
- Do they believe that their needs are being met?
- Do they respect the faculty and administrators?

Facility:
- How old is the building?
- Was it built with a specific type of curriculum in mind?
- Does it support an open environment?
- Does it support collaboration among the teachers?
- Is the building in need of repair?
- Are there plans for remodeling the school?
- Is it a new school with all of the latest innovations?

Much of the data about the school, the library media specialist will be able to obtain through observation. She will know the principal's leadership style, much of the data about the staff, and as a staff member, she will have experienced the atmosphere of the school. The school secretary can provide the student data or direct the action researcher to the person who has these figures. Some schools center this information in the guidance and counseling area or have a statistician on staff to collect this data. The library media specialist will have an idea of how the students feel about their school, but she may want to work with some of the staff members to validate her impressions. Gathering data about the facility itself may be challenging but will be an interesting search for the researcher. She should start again with the school secretary to see if there are any documents she can use to retrieve this data. The principal is also a good source to tap for this data.

The following examples illustrate how important it was for the two library media specialists to assess their environment as they were beginning their action research projects.

School Influence

Macintosh or PC: The technology committee was given funds to upgrade the computers in the library. Kris, a classroom teacher, was designated as the chairperson of this committee. She was charged with providing the committee with background information in order to make this decision. The elementary school of 600 students had mainly Macintosh computers in the classrooms, but the students had access to PC's in the library for the automated library system.

As she was gathering her data and analyzing the school, she found that the principal was a well-respected leader in the school. The principal's style was collaborative, and after he gathered information from the teachers, he would make a decision, and the staff would abide by it. As Kris analyzed the situation further, however, she found that the principal had key staff members whose opinions he respected highly. They formed his inner circle of advisors. She found that the principal respected the technology teacher and rarely questioned her suggestions. The technology teacher was a true "Mac" person. Kris discovered that the recently-hired library media specialist could also be classified as a "Mac" person. This newly-hired library media specialist was a member of the principal's advisory group. This background knowledge provided Kris with the data she needed to be aware of as she conducted her research. Assessing the school environment made her aware of the intangible influences that could affect the outcome of her research.

School Configuration: Joe was the library media specialist in a large high school that had adopted Ted Sizer's philosophy of the Coalition of Essential Schools. In order to implement this philosophy, the school had been divided into three schools with three principals, three office staffs, three faculties, and one library media specialist. The library media specialist was to work with the students, staff, and principals from all three of the schools. One can readily see the problems that this researcher would encounter. It was imperative for Joe to understand the workings of each school, the atmosphere of each school, the leadership style of each principal, and the uniqueness of each faculty. Joe needed to reflect upon the atmosphere that permeated activities when all three schools participated on a project together in order to support student learning.

The Library

Gathering information about the library can be challenging because it requires looking at the library and the library program in a very objective manner. Analyzing the library program is also an analysis of the library media specialist as a member of the library profession. Answering these questions will help the researcher reflect on her own program.

The Program:
- What values are shown through the library program?
- Is each facet of the library program dedicated to student achievement?
- Does the program reflect the library media specialist's commitment to students?
- Is the library a warm and inviting place?
- Is the program collaborative with the classroom teachers?

- Does the program reflect the national standards found in the American Association of School Librarians (AASL) and the Association for Educational Communications and Technology's (AECT), *Information Power*?
- Has the library media specialist implemented information literacy standards into the library program?
- Is there adequate library staff to implement an effective program?
- Do the faculty and staff regularly rely on the library for assistance in all phases of instruction?

The Students:
- Are students given time to access library resources for assignments?
- Does the library occasionally get so crowded that there is no room for the students needing to use the facility?
- Do students receive help when they need it?
- Have students been taught how to find materials?
- Does the library provide the students with computers, online resources, and printers to assist with homework?
- Do students like going to the library?

Teaching Staff:
- Is the curriculum of the school conducive to collaborating with the teachers?
- During collaboration with the teachers, is there a sensitivity to developing a collection that supports content standards?
- Is there a need to reassess the curriculum in order to incorporate information literacy standards?
- Do the teachers recognize the value of library resources and technologies in relation to teaching and learning?
- Do the teachers see the library media specialist as a teacher dedicated to the academic achievement of the students?

The Facility:
- Is the library facility large enough to implement a vibrant program?
- If the facility is old, is it run-down and in need of repair, or has it been well maintained?
- Is the facility conducive to learning?
- Is there a designated area for instruction?
- Are there enough electrical outlets to support the technology?
- Is the facility large enough to accommodate more than one class simultaneously?
- Is the technology infrastructure appropriate for the program?
- Is the facility located where it can provide easy access to encourage frequent use?
- Does the facility provide access for the special needs population?

Resources and Equipment:
- How old is the collection?
- Is the collection outdated or is it still a viable resource for the students?
- Does the collection support the curriculum?
- Is there an adequate budget for hardware, materials, and online resources?
- Is there adequate technical support to maintain, upgrade, and troubleshoot hardware and software needs?
- Do the faculty and staff use a wide variety of instructional resources obtained through the library?
- Is there a current selection policy?
- Is the library automated for circulating and accessing materials?

Reflection on the library and the library program by answering these questions will provide data to assist the library media specialist as she is determining the parameters of her research. This information will help determine what problems may occur as the researcher begins collecting data. The answers to the questions will provide a framework for research. The following example illustrates the necessity of answering these questions about the library prior to beginning any research.

Library Influence

Will decided he needed to evaluate database usage in his school library. There were a number of services to which his school had subscriptions, but the students and teachers were not using them. Will knew that he should implement staff development classes on the use of the databases and then determine if there were some specific services he could eliminate. Will could then re-direct those funds toward book purchases. In the data-gathering phase of his research, he learned from his principal that the library budget was going to be cut by 50% for the following year. This budgetary constraint helped him approach his action research with more immediacy.

Gathering information about the community, the school, and the library program will provide the researcher with a better knowledge of the surroundings in which she will be conducting her action research. As the researcher is obtaining these facts and opinions, she should determine which of the items will affect the research she is planning to conduct. Being aware of this data will provide a foundation of background knowledge which will assist her in developing her research project.

Collecting this data will crystallize and add to what the researcher already knows about the research environment. The data will be instrumental in developing the parameters of the project. The information will help frame the project and clarify the focus. The suggested questions listed previously are only guidelines or samples for the researcher to use. Figure 3.1 summarizes the areas that should be explored while obtaining background information.

Figure 3.1 Areas to Explore in Projects

Community	School	Library
Ethnicity	Principal	Program
Family Structure	Staff	Students
Religious values	Atmosphere	Teaching Staff
Economics	Students	Facility
Community Attitudes	Facility	Resources and Equipment
Other Resources		

Megan's Assessment of Her Environment

Megan collected the following information in her assessment of the environment.

Community: The community is economically diverse with the family income ranging from below $20,000 to over $100,000 a year. The neighborhood is well established; many homes in the immediate area of the school are older. The west end of the attendance area is a housing project of very expensive homes. There is a similar housing development on the southern border of the attendance area. There is a low-rent motel in the school attendance area which provides living places for some of the homeless students who attend Mountain Ridge. Forty percent of the families have only one parent working outside the home. This arrangement allows the other parent to volunteer at the school. Thirty percent have two working parents and 30% are from single-family homes. The average family in the Mountain Ridge attendance area has two or three children.

School: Mountain Ridge Middle School is a large middle school in a suburban area. The school has grades six, seven, and eight. The school was originally built in pods with definite divisions for each grade level. The majority of the students, 86.2%, are Caucasian and they speak English at home. The school enrollment is currently 831, which is an increase from 797 the previous year. One of the nearby housing developments is opening phase two of their project in October, and the school is expecting 50 additional students, which will bring the total enrollment close to 900 students. The majority of the students perform well on standardized tests. The attendance rate is 95.7%, which indicates that the students enjoy coming to school. The mobility rate is 11.1%, and 3% of the students are receiving free and reduced lunches.

The principal sets the tone for the school. She believes in empowering the staff and most decisions are made collaboratively. Because of her collaborative management style, the staff is fairly stable and there is a low turnover rate. The school has 48 full-time teachers and four part-time teachers. The teachers at Mountain Ridge have an average of 17 years in education. The staff is a cohesive group that supports one another both professionally and personally. The welcoming environment is evident throughout the building.

Library: The library media center is the center of the school. Walls were not built in the library media center during construction in order to maintain an open and inviting atmosphere. This arrangement makes it difficult to conduct lessons. Students and staff walk through the library media center on their way to lunch, during class changes, or simply use it as a short cut across the building. The facility is adequate at the present time, but increased enrollment will make it more difficult to provide services to all of the students. There is a full-time endorsed library media specialist plus paraprofessional help for four hours each day. The collection is in relatively good shape and is a viable resource for students. The teachers feel the curriculum is being supported through the collection at each grade level. Through collaboration, curricular needs are identified and materials are purchased to meet those goals.

Chapter Summary

In Chapter 3 we have learned that before the library media specialist begins her project, time should be spent reflecting on the current environment where the research will occur. For library-based projects the action researcher should reflect upon the library situation. For school-wide projects the library media specialist should also reflect on elements influencing the community and the school. This chapter provides an extensive list of sample questions the researcher may use to gather background information. When the library media specialist is beginning a project, this background information will provide a foundation and a means of framing the issues for the research.

4

Problem Statement to Research Question

Chapter 2 presented tips on how to determine the area which the library media specialist wants to explore through action research. Conducting the literature review provided a context in the professional literature for this topic. Chapter 3 illustrated how to examine the professional situation in the researcher's learning community. The action researcher now needs to formulate a problem statement which will help in narrowing the focus of the research and in developing the specific research questions to be explored.

Developing the Problem Statement

The first step in refining the topic is for the action researcher to brainstorm all of the possibilities of the topic. Armed with the information she has gleaned from the literature review and the exploration of the research environment, the library media specialist should wrap her mind around the topic. She must look at it from many different directions and from all angles. The researcher should ask:

- What do I really want to know about this topic?
- What am I really trying to find out?
- Does this topic support my goal of student achievement?
- What impact is this going to have on my school situation?
- Am I really passionate about this topic?
- Will the information I gather assist me in improving my professional practice?

> *Sticky note:* What impact will it have on students academic growth? How many books will go missing? How can I keep the library open for checkouts?

...cialist should pretend she is Robin Williams in the movie, *...ety*, and jump up on the desk and look around the room to ...ks from a completely different vantage point.

...dia specialist at this point should develop a problem ...mpasses the research situation. A problem statement may be ... ways. Richard Sagor in both *Guiding School Improvement* ... and *How to Conduct Collaborative Action Research* ... a graphic representation of the problem. This graphic ...researchers the opportunity to create a visual representation ...m through the use of flow charts and graphs. Farmer ...lem statement include the original topic, the affected ...d outcome, and the interventions which affect the outcome. ...in *Research for School Library Media Specialists* suggest that the researcher state the problem "as a complete sentence devoid of vague terms and jargon" (30).

Expressing the problem as a tightly-constructed statement will force the researcher to narrow the focus of the project. The statement should be a few sentences which explain the area of focus and the desired outcome. After the library media specialist has the problem statement constructed, she should begin brainstorming all possible aspects of the problem. The following examples show how Debbie and Roger developed their problem statements and then reflected on all of the circumstances of their situations.

Debbie, a library media specialist in an elementary school, was involved in the following circumstances. Her school needed an extra classroom so the computers were moved to the library and she was made responsible for both the library program and the technology program. She was concerned that this would affect the student's academic achievement since she was now acting as a library media specialist and a technology specialist. Debbie developed the following problem statement.

> **Problem statement:** *Since the population of Centennial Elementary School has increased by 50 students, the computer lab has been converted into a regular classroom. The computers have been moved to the library and the library media specialist will now be responsible for the library program and the technology program. I need to explore the impact this change may have on the achievement level of the students at Centennial.*

Debbie then brainstormed with a professional colleague, and developed the following questions.

- Will moving the computer lab into the library impact the students' academic achievement?
- To what extent will having the computer lab in the library impact library instruction?
- If the library media specialist is working in the computer lab, how many students will come to the library and leave without having the benefit of

working with the library media specialist to choose a special book?
- Will having the library media specialist responsible for the computers change her image from librarian to technology specialist?
- To what extent do the benefits of having 30 computers outweigh the constraints on the physical space in the library?
- Will having the computer lab in the library impact the library media specialist's planning time with teachers?
- Will this arrangement now allow the teachers to view the library as a "drop and run" area where the teachers leave their students and use the time as planning time?

Debbie's brainstorming allowed her to put on paper all of the questions she could think of which related to her problem. From this brainstorming, she can decide which questions really focus on the information she wants to obtain.

Roger, library media specialist in a middle school, was familiar with the Accelerated Reading (AR) program being used effectively in some schools in his district at the elementary level. Some of his fellow staff members were pressuring him to implement this program at their middle school. Roger developed the following problem statement.

> **Problem statement**: *The AR program has been used successfully at our feeder elementary schools. Some of our staff members have suggested that we implement this program at our middle school. I need to know if this program will help the students increase their reading ability.*

During Roger's brainstorming, he asked himself these questions.

- Is AR an effective reading program for middle schools students?
- Will implementing AR help the students' academic achievement?
- What are the ramifications of using this program in our middle school?
- Will the teachers and students begin to rely on this program too much?
- Are there other middle schools where AR is being used successfully?
- Do the teachers and the library media specialist at those schools think that this is an effective and successful program?
- Will student test scores improve with the implementation of AR?
- Will the students' independent reading increase if they actively participate in AR?
- Will AR promote or impact our Sustained Silent Reading Program?

Roger approached his brainstorming as if the problem were a Rubic's Cube, looking at all different sides of the problem and the combinations which would provide him with the information needed to make a sound decision about implementing the program.

This initial brainstorming is crucial in identifying all of the facets of the question to be explored. This brainstorming will assist the action researcher with determining all aspects of the focus area. It is also very effective to have a colleague participate in this brainstorming to generate additional ideas. The library media specialist may want to organize a focus group consisting of teachers on her staff or other library media specialists. A focus group would provide additional questions which the researcher may not have considered. After reflecting on these ideas, the action researcher needs to narrow the focus and develop one or two questions which will pinpoint the desired action.

Developing the Research Question

After developing a problem statement and brainstorming all aspects of the educational problem, it is time to narrow the focus by developing the specific research question(s) the library media specialist will be using to collect data. One trap that some researchers fall into is deciding what data collection techniques they will use without developing the focused research questions. It is easy to think that the researcher can do interviews, develop a survey, and observe the students, but if the researcher skips the step of developing the questions, the action research project will become more difficult as the researcher begins the data collection. We can not stress the point enough. The action researcher must take the time to analyze the problem, brainstorm the issue, and develop the questions which will steer the researcher in the direction of evaluating any desired changes.

Research questions should be open-ended. Hubbard and Power in *The Art of Classroom Inquiry* indicate that the questions should be open-ended enough to permit the researcher to discover possibilities which she had not even considered. Having a question that can be answered with a "yes" or a "no" may be used when gathering quantitative data but will be detrimental to collecting descriptive qualitative data. The questions should be written so that data collected describes the situation. Having descriptive data allows the library media specialist to ascertain the current situation so that she is able to implement a plan for improvement. Questions which will elicit this data should be "What" or "How" questions.

The following are sample research questions:

- What procedures or activities promote or encourage students to read more books?
- How does a flexible schedule affect student achievement?
- What acquisitions or materials are needed to support the new fifth grade science curriculum?
- How much academic growth can be expected with regular instruction through the library program?
- What parameters need to be explored before implementing a library automation system?
- How will subscribing to online databases impact student achievement?
- What library services are necessary for a successful high school library program?
- How do teachers and students currently view the laptops as a resource?
- What happens if the circulation period is changed from two weeks to four weeks?
- How can I develop a collaborative atmosphere in the school?

- How does Sustained Silent Reading impact students' love of reading?
- What is the difference between a fixed schedule and a flexible schedule in relation to student achievement?
- What software is currently useful to teachers and students in meeting curriculum needs?
- What instruction is needed to increase the use of online databases?
- How does using Spanish with second-language learners impact their academic achievement?
- What strategies should I use to develop the ethical use of the Internet in my library?

Each of these questions begins with either "What" or "How" and will allow the library media specialist to gather descriptive data.

Looking back at Debbie's brainstorming, what research question can she use to target the collection of the data she needs? She wants to find out if moving the computer lab into the library and assuming the role of library media specialist and technology specialist will affect student achievement. Her brainstorming looked at all different sides of the issue. Debbie composed the following research question. *How will moving the computer lab into the library affect the students' academic achievement?* After she reviewed all of her brainstorming questions, she decided that this was what she really wanted to know. The other questions are imbedded in this one. She can now begin collecting data.

Roger needs to decide whether he should implement AR in his middle school. Looking at his problem statement and his brainstorming, he developed the following research question. *What will be the effect on student achievement of implementing the Accelerated Reader program at the middle-school level?*

Both Debbie and Roger followed a specific process. They took their focus areas, developed problem statements, brainstormed the issues from all sides, and then narrowed their focus to one research question which they can now use to begin collecting data.

Developing the research question is not a difficult process, but it takes a certain amount of reflection and analysis to make certain the library media specialist is clear about what she is trying to accomplish through action research. If this process is not completed in a reflective manner, problems will occur as the researcher delves into the action research process. The researcher must take the time to be assured she is on the right road to end up at the expected destination.

Megan's Problem Statement:

The library program must be a well-developed program in which students are learning to be independent library users as well as benefiting from instruction received at the point of need through flexible scheduling.

Brainstorming questions:

- Are the teachers using the library and the library media specialist as a resource when planning lessons?
- Will I be used as a resource when planning curricular lessons?
- How can I be sure that the library program is supporting student achievement?
- Do teachers view the library and information literacy standards as a natural part of the curriculum?
- Am I effectively connecting with teachers to collaborate and plan thoughtful lessons that complement grade-level curriculum?
- Are information literacy standards being implemented effectively through the flexible schedule?
- As I collaborate with teachers, am I continually referring back to information literacy standards, fulfilling them through the lessons we develop?
- Are teachers aware of information literacy standards and do they see a need to implement them into lessons?
- Are students becoming independent library users?
- Do students feel they can come into the library at any given time and be able to find the information they need?
- Do they feel comfortable in the library and not overwhelmed or intimidated?
- Are students and staff comfortable using an online database to search for information?
- Without a scheduled library time, are all students coming to the library and checking out books or is there a portion of the population that is not being served?
- Is the flexible schedule meeting the needs of the library staff?
- Am I finding enough time to thoughtfully plan lessons with classroom teachers?
- Am I able to meet with every class on a regular basis to teach information literacy standards?
- Does my library clerk feel overwhelmed since I am not able to help her with circulation of materials?

From this problem statement and brainstorming activity, Megan developed the following research questions:

1. How are students learning to be independent library learners through the new flexible schedule?
2. How is the flexible schedule making an impact on student learning?

Chapter Summary

In Chapter 4 we have learned how to progress from a problem statement to a research question. The problem statement should be two to three sentences that clearly narrow the area of focus and state the desired outcome. The researcher then needs to brainstorm all possible questions relating to the topic. Through this brainstorming the library media specialist will be able to determine what question she really wants to answer. The question should be framed as a "how" or "why" inquiry. This question will be the focus of her research.

5

Collecting Data

Once the library media specialist is comfortable with narrowing her research through developing focused research questions, she must then decide how she is going to collect and analyze the data. In order to assure validity and reliability, the library media specialist should triangulate the data. Collecting data from just one source could provide the researcher with results that may not reflect the true scenario. Collecting data from more than one source and analyzing that data will give a more accurate picture of the reality of the situation. When conducting action research, it is a general practice to use three different methods to collect the data in search of answers for each question. The triangulation matrix shown in Figure 5.1 illustrates how one library media specialist used three different methods for each question she was exploring.

Fig. 5.1. Triangulation Matrix.

Research question	Data Source #1	Data Source #2	Data Source #3
How does the present schedule account for lessons being taught at the time of need?	Survey of staff	Survey of students	Analysis of unfilled library requests.
Which teachers are unable to participate in collaborative planning because of the current schedule?	Survey of staff	Interviews with grade level chairs	Analysis of unscheduled library time.
How does the present schedule accommodate the student's need for reader's advisory?	Survey of staff	Interviews with random sample of students	Interviews with random sample of parents.

Data Collection Tools

There are various tools which the library media specialist may use in order to collect data. Schmuck, Sagor (*Guiding, How*), Johnson, and Mills all provide good examples of how to collect data. Some of the most frequently used data collection tools are: questionnaires, interviews, observations with journal entries, and archival sources.

Questionnaires

One of the most popular forms of collecting data is through the use of a questionnaire, often referred to as a survey. For our purposes, we will use the two terms interchangeably. Questionnaires are a quick and easy way to gather information from many different people. A survey can be administered in a short amount of time. Surveys should not take more than 10 to 15 minutes for the respondent to complete. Researchers can administer the questionnaires in a face-to-face manner or via electronic means. Different types of questions may be included in the surveys. Sagor indicates that surveys allow the researcher to ask cognitive, attitudinal, and affective types of questions depending on how the researcher structures the inquiry. (*Guiding*) The researcher should decide which type of question is most effective to use to obtain the information she needs. She may also use all three types of questions to gain the appropriate information. While surveying just one group of students working in the library, the library media specialist could ask:

- How many books do you have checked out? (Cognitive)
- What do you think about the arrangement of the easy chairs in the library? (Attitudinal)
- How do you feel about spending your study period in the library? (Affective)

Questionnaires may include a variety of formats. The library media specialist may use open-ended or closed-response questions. Open-ended questions allow the respondents an opportunity to express their answers using their own words.

- When you come to the library, what is your favorite activity?
- What books would you like the library to purchase?

Another type of open-ended question asks the respondent to provide a list of items which answer the question. The question might be:

- What three library activities do you like the best?
- What are your three favorite books?

These types of questions allow the respondent to decide the most appropriate answers and does not confine them to a specific set of choices. The library media specialist may glean unexpected information from the answers to these types of questions. Open-ended questions such as these are easy to develop and will provide the library media specialist with a wealth of qualitative information.

Closed-response questions may use a Likert scale which allows the respondents to select their answers from a series of choices. The common choices are: strongly agree (SA), agree (A), undecided (U), disagree (D), strongly disagree

(SD). The respondent shows how she feels about a certain issue by choosing the degree which reflects her thinking. As the library media specialist is developing the surveys, she must determine the number of choices for answers. If she uses an even number of choices, she is forcing the respondent to make a choice of a positive response or a negative response. When using an odd number of choices, then the respondent's answer can be neutral. Some researchers use an attitude scale having two opposite terms with varying degrees in between. The student then indicates where on the scale her thinking is.

Sad — / — / — / — / — / — / — Happy

Easy — / — / — / — / — / — / — Hard

Boring — / — / — / — / — / — / — Fun

The person completing the questionnaire would indicate whether her thinking was closer to happy or closer to sad. Elementary library media specialists may use a series of faces, happy ones on one end of the spectrum and sad faces on the other. Offering visual representations allow younger students to use familiar symbols to record their responses.

The library media specialist should also determine if there is a need to ask for background information at the beginning of the survey. The action researcher needs to decide if she will ask the respondent to identify herself or if the survey will be completed anonymously. The researcher should also determine if there will be a need to disaggregate the data after it is collected. Disaggregating the data allows the researcher to examine the data by looking at different subsets. If the researcher needs to look at all of the surveys from a specific class, at a specific grade level, or by gender, then that information needs to be accounted for on the survey. This data can be collected by having a place for the teacher's name, the grade level, or through indicating whether the person is male or female.

When developing the questions for the survey, the library media specialist should guard against asking questions which will elicit the response she wants instead of determining what the situation really is. The researcher must guard against using leading questions. If the researcher wants to determine if the library is seen as a friendly, inviting place, then she should ask: *What word describes how you feel when you come to the library?* and not *How do you know that the library is a friendly place*? Using the first question will allow the respondent to share her feelings with the library media specialist. Using the second question assumes that the respondent already thinks that the library is a friendly place. It is leading the respondent down the path the researcher has determined instead of ascertaining what the respondent believes.

Even though questionnaires are a good way to collect data, there are some difficulties with using this data collection tool. When analyzing the open-ended responses, the answers may be ambiguous because of the words the respondents used. A significant amount of time is necessary to analyze the responses to this type of question because of the volume of information provided. Using terms such as "happy" and "sad" as rating scales may provide unclear answers since different

Chapter Five: Collecting Data

people interpret being happy or being sad differently. When using closed-response questions, the data collector is not able to have the respondent clarify her answer. The data collector does not have the opportunity to establish a rapport with the respondent since the survey is given to a large group at the same time.

If the library media specialist has a survey that is being given to a large group of students, she might consider using an electronic survey tool which can be found by searching the Internet. These Web sites allow the researcher to develop the survey, send it to a specific number of respondents, have the respondents complete the survey, and then the survey tool tabulates the results. In this age of accountability, some school districts are subscribing to this type of service to assist in gathering data. The researcher should check to see if one of these sources is available for her use. Some of the sources allow a short survey to be developed and used without charge. Two of the commonly used survey tools are Zoomerang and Survey Monkey. The library media specialist should explore the possibility of using one of these resources and then determine which tool will best fit her needs. NPower has published an online report comparing eight of these electronic tools. They have included a comparison chart that will provide the action researcher the data needed to decide if using one of these tools is conducive to her research. Figure 5.2 illustrates the advantages and disadvantages of questionnaires.

Fig. 5.2. Advantages and Disadvantages of Questionnaires. Adapted from Schmuck (54).

Advantages	Disadvantages
Open-ended questions are easily created.	Open-ended responses can be ambiguous.
Respondents can complete them quickly.	Analyzing open-ended responses takes much time.
Open-ended questions provide rich quotations that are useful for data feedback.	If questions with rating scales include two or more ideas, the results will be unclear.
The researcher is able to learn unexpected information if allowing for more than one answer for the question. (What three things do you like….?)	The researcher cannot clarify the respondent's answers.
Rating scales allow for quick scoring and development of graphs to display data.	The researcher does not have the opportunity to establish rapport with the respondent.

Helpful Tips

The following tips will help the library media specialist in preparing surveys:

- Limit the survey to 10 or 15 questions.
- Create the survey so that it can be completed in 15 minutes or less.
- Proofread the survey to eliminate any mistakes.
- Pilot the survey with a small group to insure the questions asked provide the needed answers.
- Provide an opportunity to let the respondent express any ideas she chooses to by having a comments section.

Megan's Survey

Megan developed the following survey to gather information from the students. Notice that she has only eight questions and that she provides a place for comments.

Directions: Please answer the following questions by circling your response.

1. How often do you ask to go to the library?
   a. Once a month
   b. Twice a month
   c. Once a week
   d. Twice a week
   e. Almost every day

2. Why do you come to the library? _____

3. Are you able to find books in the library by yourself?
   ____ Yes   ____ No   ____ Sometimes   ____ I am still learning how

4. When you come to the library, how do you find books? (Place a checkmark by the thing you do first.)
   ____ I ask the librarian for help.
   ____ I ask the teacher for help.
   ____ I look on the shelves.
   ____ I go to the computer.
   ____ I ask a friend for help.
   ____ Other

5. How well do you know how to use the library computers to find books?
   ____ I am a pro at it.
   ____ I can usually find what I am looking for.
   ____ I do not really understand how to use it, but I will try.
   ____ I have no idea how to use it, but I'd like to learn.
   ____ I have no idea how to use it and I don't care.

6. How comfortable do you feel in the library?
   ____ I love the library.
   ____ I like going to the library.
   ____ The library is okay.
   ____ I hate going to the library.

7. Are you able to go to the library as much as you want while you are at school?
   ____ Yes   ____ No   ____ Most times

8. What have you learned in the library or in the computer lab with Ms. Jones this year? (Check all that apply)
   ____ About the dictionary
   ____ How to use the computers to find books
   ____ How to use the electronic database
   ____ How to use the computer for research
   ____ How to use the library for research
   ____ Presentation software
   ____ Electronic books on the computer
   ____ Genres
   ____ Five finger rule
   ____ How to choose a good book
   ____ Using a word processor

Chapter Five: Collecting Data

Interviews

Interviews and questionnaires have various characteristics in common. Both interviews and questionnaires should be developed to include closed-response and open-ended questions. Both should guard against leading questions. Both interviews and surveys should have only 10 to 15 questions. When using interviews, the researcher is able to ask clarifying questions to make certain she understands the respondent's answer. The researcher is able to develop a rapport with the interviewee during the interview process. This rapport may assist the researcher in gaining information which would not be available through a questionnaire.

Two other items need to be considered before the library media specialist uses interviews as a means of data collection. The anonymity of the interviewee is eliminated and sometimes the respondent will answer more truthfully if her identity is kept secret. If the students being interviewed do not know the interviewer, developing the necessary rapport may be difficult. The logistics of interviewing must be considered. A private area should be used to conduct the interview and in a busy school situation, finding such a place might be difficult. Conducting an interview takes a considerable amount of time compared to administering a questionnaire. Sagor states that interviews should not last longer than a maximum of 45 minutes. (*Guiding*)

The researcher should also consider how she will collect the data. During interviews, as clarifying questions are asked, additional information that is not part of the interview "script" will be gathered. The library media specialist should determine how this data will be handled. The researcher should take notes during the interview but should be attuned to how comfortable the interviewee is. To focus more on the person being interviewed, the library media specialist may want to have another person at the interview to keep track of what the respondent is saying. The researcher is then able to concentrate on the person being interviewed. The library media specialist may decide to use an audiotape or a videotape of the session to eliminate taking notes during the actual interview. The researcher must build time into the process to evaluate these tapes. It is important to remember that to evaluate a 45-minute session, the library media specialist will need at least an additional 45 minutes.

Another interview technique is to use group interviews. This process allows the library media specialist to collect more responses at one time. A problem could occur with the interview technique if the person who initially answers the question unduly influences the group of respondents. The researcher may want to use a focus group as another form of a group interview. The focus group is a more structured setting where the researcher has a series of open-ended questions that she asks in order to stimulate a group discussion. During this discussion, the focus group will attempt to synthesize the questions and solidify the answers for the researcher. An interview is a good source of collecting data if the researcher is aware of the limitations. Figure 5.3 lists the advantages and disadvantages of interviews as a data-collection tool.

Fig. 5.3. Advantages and Disadvantages of Interviews. Adapted from Schmuck (55).

Advantages	Disadvantages
The researcher is able to probe for clarification and elaboration.	Interviews are time consuming.
The researcher is able to build rapport with the respondents.	The researcher will need to use sampling techniques if she is not able to interview everyone or is using group interviews.
The researcher is able to collect information from respondents who would not fill out a questionnaire.	With individual interviews, the respondent is no longer anonymous.
If pooling answers in groups, the respondents can remain anonymous.	The researcher may unintentionally cause bias in the respondent's answers.

The following example shows how one library media specialist used an interview to gather needed information.

Gifted and Talented Magnet School: The elementary school where Randy has just been hired as a library media specialist is being reconfigured and will be a magnet school for gifted and talented students. Randy realizes that he does not have the necessary materials in the library to help the students and the teaching staff. Although he plans to eventually survey the students to find out what they need as resources, he decided it would be better to first interview the staff about their projected needs. He asked the following five questions to collect the information he desired.

1. What are the gaps or shortcomings of the library as far as meeting the needs of the gifted and talented students in our building?
2. What upcoming units do you have that will require additional materials from our library?
3. Will you be emphasizing non-fiction materials or fiction materials in your classes?
4. What kinds of books would you like to see in the library?
5. What specific genres will you be requiring your students to study?

Randy then made the commitment to interview each of the 20 classroom teachers before the end of the first nine weeks to collect the data he would need to realign the collection to the new gifted and talented population. He made appointments with the teachers during their planning periods. Since he felt the teachers would be comfortable with him asking the questions, he kept track of the teachers' responses. Each interview was completed in an average of 30 minutes. Randy gathered incredible data during these interviews and now has a good idea of how to develop the collection. He was able to glean much more information from the teachers through the individual interviews than he would have been able to gather through surveys. He also began to establish strong connections with the faculty.

Chapter Five: Collecting Data

Observations

A third source of collecting data is through observing the setting which relates to the research question. Observations may be conducted in a variety of ways depending on the types of data which the observer wishes to collect. The library media specialist may observe a situation where she is either completely involved in the activity or where she is only a witness to what is occurring. Vicki wanted to observe which databases the students accessed first when they were conducting research in the library. She stationed herself at the reference area so that she could interact with the students as they began accessing the databases. She was there to answer questions if the students had any and was also able to determine how the students conducted their searches. Vicki acted as an active participant in the observations.

Mills describes a passive observer as another way to make observations. Teri wanted to observe which part of the library the students accessed when they first arrived. She was determining if the traffic flow in the library was conducive to the students having access to the library automation system. She did not want to influence the students or interact with them in any way. She simply wanted to observe the traffic patterns. Therefore, Teri made certain she was able to observe the student activity without being available to interact with them.

Sagor encourages the researcher to use two different methods of collecting data through observations. (*Guiding*) The library media specialist may use an open-ended checklist or one with predefined terms. An **open-ended checklist** allows the researcher to create the checklist as the action is occurring. The observer begins with a blank sheet of paper and lists what happens during the time period of the observation. If the students check out books, the observer adds that to her list. If the students are engaged in research, the observer adds this activity to the checklist. If the students are browsing in the stacks, the observer adds this item to the list. If any of these activities occur a second time, the researcher indicates the occurrence with a hash mark on the list. When using an open-ended checklist, the library media specialist must determine what specific terms mean. For example, what does "engage" in research mean? Does it mean the students are sitting at the table and taking notes? Does it mean they are working quietly without interacting with their peers or the library media specialist? Does it mean that the students are accessing online databases? Having these terms defined will assist the library media specialist in knowing how to tabulate the actions as they unfold.

The **predefined checklist** has the observer looking for specific actions and only those actions. The library media specialist will begin this observational period using a list of actions that she will try to find. Maybe she wants to know how many students sit at the tables, how many search the stacks, how many use the computers during a certain snapshot of time. She will then tabulate the students' actions for a predetermined amount of time and record the number of times she observes this action.

A third way to collect observational data is to sit in the library for a specific time period and simply record what actions are occurring. The library media specialist will allocate a class period or 15 to 20 minutes, and simply write what she notices happening. Using a free-flowing journal allows the action researcher to record the actions occurring and also the subjective conclusions she has made during this snapshot. Figure 5.4 identifies the advantages and the disadvantages of using observations.

| Fig. 5.4. Advantages and Disadvantages of Observations. Adapted from Schmuck (55). ||
Advantages	**Disadvantages**
Researcher is able to gather data about behaviors rather than just about perceptions and feelings.	The researcher's presence may alter the respondent's behavior.
The researcher may see things that some respondents will not be able to report.	The researcher might have to wait a long time before seeing what she seeks to observe.
Data can be gathered by videotaping to study later.	Different researchers might see different things while observing the same events.

The following is an example of how Kathy used observation as a data collection tool.

Appropriate Database: Kathy, the library media specialist at George Reed Middle School, wanted to know if the students were able to access the library's databases successfully after their initial introduction to the sources. She spent three class periods observing the students using the databases to determine if they were able to access the information they needed. Kathy recorded her observations in her journal. The following is one of her journal entries: *After introducing the databases to the seventh and ninth grade social studies classes, I spent the next two class periods observing their research behaviors. When the students of all grades were using the first database, they displayed no frustrations, seemed to be able to navigate the sites quickly, and stayed on the sites long enough to take the needed notes. Two boys said they preferred using a particular book on Ireland that had a copyright date of 1993. When I had them compare the information to the database, they found some information that was more current. However, they liked how the book gave them more information about the customs. When the seventh grade students attempted to use the second database, I noticed them asking their teachers many questions about how to find their country. One teacher also had difficulty navigating the site. This shows me that I need to present more information, hands-on lessons, and practice on how to use this database. The students in these two classes seem to be able to use the first database fairly easily.*

Kathy was trying to discover the success of her introductory lessons and whether she needed to provide additional training. Through this one observation of the two classes, she gathered helpful data to begin answering her question. She needs to continue with her observations to see if she finds the same results. If she conducts further observations with other classes and arrives at the same conclusion, then she will have a clear picture of how effective her presentations were and where more teaching needs to occur.

Archival Information

Another means of data collection an action researcher may use is gathering the wealth of archival information found in schools. Archival data includes the cumulative folders for each of the students, electronic databases containing student test data, and student records containing ethnic data. Other sources of data available to the library media specialist are the circulation statistics for the library disaggregated by class, gender, or time period; the library schedule containing the number of classes coming to the library; the subject areas taught; and the types of lessons the library media specialist has presented. These are only a few of the archival records which may be used as sources of data. When using student data, the researcher must be aware of the protocol of the school and follow those procedures. When using archival data, the confidentiality of student records both through the student data system and the circulation records must be upheld.

These are the most common means of collecting data that are available for the action researcher to use in gathering information. The researcher should determine which methods are most appropriate to use to gather needed data. The researcher must consider the research questions, the time line, and the available data as she chooses the methods to use for a project.

The matrix shown in Figure 5.5 illustrates the data sources Megan used to collect information.

Fig. 5.5. Megan's Data Collection Sources.

Research Question	Data Source #1	Data Source #2	Data Source #3
How are students learning to be independent library learners through the new flexible schedule?	Student Survey	Observation of Students in Library	Staff Survey
How is the flexible schedule making an impact on student learning?	Student Survey	Journal with Observations	Staff Survey

Chapter Summary

In Chapter 5 we explored the most common data-collection tools. These tools include questionnaires, interviews, observations, and archival information. Questionnaires are used to collect a large amount of information very quickly. Interviews allow the library media specialist to ask clarifying questions and to probe the subject more deeply and thoroughly. The action researcher may conduct observations as either a participant or as a passive observer. Archival sources also present the action researcher with a wealth of information when specific data about groups or individual student needs is required. There are positives and negatives for using each of these data collection methods. The library media specialist needs to evaluate each tool and determine which tools are best suited for her research application.

6

Planning Considerations

While the library media specialist determines the most appropriate method of collecting data, she must also consider the following factors: generalizability, validity, and reliability. If the information is valid, the researcher knows that the data collected answers the questions the researcher is asking. Data are reliable if the same questions elicit the same answers even though respondents are different. Generalizability addresses the function of replicating the study in different locations while still achieving the same results.

Generalizability

Generalizability is the quality of research that allows the researcher to replicate the study in a different situation and arrive at the same conclusion. In traditional studies, the researcher will consider generalizability as she is conducting her study with more than one group. Generalizability is the result of statistical analysis and sample selection. In traditional studies the researcher uses parts or samples of a population to represent the entire population. Keith Curry Lance has replicated his studies concerning the effectiveness of library media centers in relation to higher student achievement in more than one state with the same results. His studies show generalizability. He has used a statistical plan and sample selection to discover tendencies which can then be applied to the whole population. Generalizability is not a characteristic of action research projects, since the library media specialist is concerned with improvement through reflective practice in her own school situation. She is collecting data, both quantitative and qualitative, that will describe the problem at her school alone.

Validity

Validity refers to the truthfulness in the data that are collected. Does the data I collect answer the question I am asking? Are there other factors that might influence whether the data I have collected are giving me the true information I want? Farmer describes a situation in which a library media specialist wants to explore a student's reading habits. In this case, collecting statistical data on the number of books the student checks out could give misleading information. Just because a student checks a book out does not prove she reads it. She might be checking the book out for a friend or she might be reading books from other sources besides the library media center. Collecting the circulation statistics would not be a valid source to determine the reading habits of students. Circulation statistics can be used to determine if the library collection is being utilized more frequently from one year to the next.

Reliability

Reliability addresses the accuracy of the data that are collected. Educators are familiar with the concept of reliability through their experiences in administering standardized tests. Companies producing these tests provide instructions for the proctor of the test to make certain the test will be a reliable measurement of the student's ability. In action research, if two or more researchers are collecting data, they need to make certain they are each collecting the data in the same manner. If both are conducting interviews, both must brainstorm how they will conduct these interviews to make certain they gather reliable data. Will the interviewer ask follow-up questions? How will the interviewer handle an interrupted interview? Having both interviewers decide how they will conduct the interview will assist in gathering consistently reliable data.

Sagor provides questions a researcher may use to be aware of validity and reliability.

- *Validity*: "Are there any factors or intervening variables that should cause me to distrust these data?" (*Guiding* 111)
- *Reliability*: "Is this information an accurate representation of reality?" "Can I think of any reasons to be suspicious of its accuracy?" (*Guiding* 112)

Another way to think of validity and reliability is to consider one's bathroom scale. The scale is a *valid* source of information for a person's weight. The scale has been calibrated with certain standards and should provide the same results for the person using the scale unless the person's weight changes because of eating too much or not enough. The scale is also a *reliable* source of information for a person trying to determine her weight. The scale is both a valid and a reliable source. The reliability of the scale may be questioned, however, if the same person weighs less when the scale is placed in a certain area of the room, or on a certain type of floor material, or if the battery needs to be changed. Each of these situations could affect the reliability of the scale. The scale may still give valid information but not reliable information if the position of the scale affects the results.

Reliability may be affected by the sample size collected for the project. If the library media specialist tries to determine the success of her school-wide program and only asks the second graders who have been using the library on a regular basis and have participated in a wide variety of positive experiences, then this would not be reliable data because the sample size included only one grade level. Do the fifth graders who have not used the library for more than a weekly book checkout feel the same? To gather reliable data concerning a school-wide program, all grade levels must be surveyed. In this instance the action researcher may have a population which would be too large to handle without using a sample of the population. To determine a reliable sample size, the library media specialist may want to use a sample size calculator which is located at various Web sites on the Internet. In order to use such a calculator, the action researcher needs to determine the **confidence interval** and the **confidence level**. The confidence interval is the + or – figure which we often see in television and radio polls. These signs refer to how accurate the sample size is in relation to the whole population. For example a confidence interval of + or – three means that the sample size is accurate within a range of three points higher or lower than the entire population. The confidence level tells how the answers from the sample population may be interpreted for the entire population. Most researchers use a confidence level of 95%. The library media specialist should use the sample size calculator if she has a large population in her study or if she has had difficulty in retrieving the data from her respondents. Using the calculator will give her a good idea about how reliable her samples are, given the number of responses she has received.

The library media specialist must account for both reliability and validity in collecting the data. Two other criteria that should be considered are personal bias and ethics. Like reliability and validity, the researcher must reflect upon her personal biases and personal ethics before she proceeds with data collection.

Personal Bias

Library media specialists need to strive for objectivity while conducting action research projects. Because the research is being conducted in one's own professional surroundings, sometimes this is difficult. It may be hard to distinguish between validating one's own beliefs and actually accepting what the data tell the researcher. Nita, a library media specialist at a K-5 school, was asked by her principal to organize a team to collect data on whether an extended-day kindergarten should be implemented at the school in order to better prepare the students to enter the first grade. Nita and two other teachers on the team had their own children in an extended day kindergarten, and all three of them believed that this was the reason for their children's success in the first grade. The team collected data from two neighboring schools that had the extended-day program and compared it with the students at their school where the program had not been implemented. After analyzing the data, the team found that there was not any clear-cut evidence that the extended day kindergarten contributed to the students' success in the first grade. Nita and her team had to put their biases aside and analyze the data objectively.

In order to guard against personal bias, the library media specialist should reflect upon the topic being researched and note her own personal ideas concerning the topic. Schmuck addresses this situation in the steps he outlines in his proactive action research. After the researcher incorporates a new practice, she should list what she hopes will occur through the process and she should indicate what concerns she has with the process. If the researcher reflects on both hopes and concerns, she will be more cognizant of any possible personally-skewed point of view which might occur. Anticipating the area of personal views will help the action researcher guard against biases affecting the action research project.

Personal Ethics

Each of us has our own set of personal values and ethics which are guiding principles in our lives. As the library media specialist is preparing her data collection tools, she must take time to reflect upon how she will handle any data she collects if it could prove embarrassing or uncomfortable if the data were made public.

Kim, one of two library media specialists at a large high school, was asked by the head library media specialist to evaluate the entire library program including how she, the head librarian, interacts with the staff members. Kim realized from previous interactions with the staff that the data collected could be both negative and positive. Sharing the negative data with the head library media specialist could be uncomfortable. Kim had a frank discussion with the head library media specialist before he gathered the data to determine what should be done with the results.

Ethics may also come into play when the action researcher is analyzing the collected data and comparing it with the information gleaned from the literature review. The action researcher must account for all sides of the information that has been collected, whether it agrees with the professional literature or not. Eliminating data because it does not "fit" with the conclusions the researcher is hoping to find would negate the value of conducting the research.

When the action researcher is examining her own values and ethics, she must also consider the participants in the action research project. Some staff members would like to remain anonymous when completing a questionnaire. If they are uncomfortable with the questions or the subject area, they may decide to forego completing the survey if their identities are not protected. The researcher must determine if she will respect this anonymity or whether to eliminate that person as a possible respondent.

Another area of ethics to consider is the interaction the researcher has with the students. Each school district has a protocol to be used when gathering information from students whether it is through video or audio taping, interviews, or surveys. The researcher must be aware of district procedures and follow them to the letter. The action researcher must align her professional ethics with her personal ethics and values in order to have a viable action research project.

Timeline

The next step in the action research process is for the library media specialist to create a timeline. This timeline is a blueprint which shows when each aspect of the research project will be accomplished and the schedule for completing various tasks associated with the project. The timeline is an overall view of all the component parts of the research. Johnson provides a concise *Checklist for Collecting Data*. The researcher should develop a similar checklist or timeline which will give an overview of the entire project. This timeline should include the following:

- The dates, times, places, and participants for data instruments being used: surveys, observations, interviews, journaling, and archival information.
- The dates and times:
    the data will be analyzed.
    for collecting any follow-up data.
    the project will be completed.
    any follow-up action will be implemented.
    the results of the research will be shared with the staff or other key parties.

Peer Review

The library media specialist will now feel comfortable that the project can be accomplished in the designated time. One last step remains before the action researcher should begin the data collection. The action researcher should take the timeline she has developed and share this with a few of her colleagues. If the library media specialist is already working with a group, then this is not as necessary because they have been sharing ideas throughout the project. If the researcher is working by herself, it will assist her in gaining a good perspective by sharing her outline with other interested parties.

This peer review should be a collaborative discussion of the logic and feasibility of the whole project. The library media specialist should share the background, review the problem statement, and discuss the overall design of the study and what she hopes to accomplish through the research. The action researcher should discuss the participants and share the triangulation matrix with her review team. The review team should look at the data collection instruments the library media specialist has developed and be certain that the questions she has created will answer the questions she is trying to address. The action researcher should explain how she will be analyzing the data and the timeline for implementing any new strategies based on her research. She should be frank about her expectations for the outcome of her project and about any negative or positive outcomes that might occur because of her research. Finally, she needs to share how and when she will present this information to the staff. This peer review will help the action researcher identify changes that should be implemented prior to beginning the project. This process will assist in solidifying the conceptualization of the project.

Megan's Timeline

(The following is a portion of Megan's Timeline)

October 1	Begin flexible schedule.
November 14	Explain procedures to staff at staff meeting.
November 15	Administer surveys to Johnson's seventh grade, seventh period.
November 16	Administer surveys to Hill's sixth grade, third period.
November 16	Observe McDermott's sixth grade class during period four.
November 22	Observe Smith's eighth grade class during first period.
November 28	Survey staff at staff meeting.
December 1	Contact staff who have not returned survey.
December 8	Code data and interpret results.
January 5	Present findings to principal.
January 7	Present findings to staff at staff meeting.
January 24	Implement complete flexible schedule for library.

Chapter Summary

In Chapter 6 we have discussed the issues of generalizability, validity, reliability, personal ethics, and personal bias. The library media specialist is not concerned with generalizability but must account for the validity and reliability of her project. As she is organizing her action research, she must be aware of her own personal ethics to make certain she collects the data in an objective manner. After the action researcher has examined these issues, she must develop a timeline for the events and form a blueprint for the project. The last step prior to collecting the data is to present her overall plan to a few of her colleagues to make certain her project is logical, possible, and feasible.

7

Organizing and Interpreting Data

Following the timeline the library media specialist has established, she should collect the necessary data. She may need to make adjustments because of unexpected events which have occurred in the daily schedule. If, for instance, some students are going on a field trip and the researcher was unaware of this occurrence, then the schedule should be adjusted. The researcher should protect the validity and reliability of the data by making sure any substituted participants will maintain the integrity of the process. If the library media specialist is looking at one class from each grade level and the second graders are unable to participate in the process, then the researcher should ask another second-grade class to participate.

Coding the Data

Once all the data are collected, then the fun begins. The researcher now needs to code the data. Coding is organizing the data into meaningful sets, piles, or categories so that it will be easy to interpret the findings. Depending on how the action researcher has organized her project, both quantitative data and qualitative data need to be organized. Quantitative data should be tabulated using a chart or a matrix. Gustafson and Smith provide a coding form that will assist the researcher. They also provide detailed instructions on how to use this form. The action researcher needs a method, whether it is a form similar to Gustafson and Smith's, an electronic chart or graph, or simply a piece of paper where the responses may be tabulated. The library media specialist should take each survey and list the number of times that a specific question is answered the same. For example, the researcher should record the number of times the respondents answer question one with "strongly agrees." The library media specialist needs to keep track by hash marks so that the total number of responses will be tabulated. The library media specialist will then proceed to each possible choice and perform a similar tabulation. For example, Dan gave the students a survey to determine which library lessons were the most helpful. One statement he posed on his survey was: "I learned how to use the online research data base to find magazine articles." The students were able to respond by choosing, "A. Strongly Agree; B. Agree; C. Disagree; D. Strongly Disagree; or E. Absent." He surveyed forty-four students and tabulated the following results:

A.	Strongly agree	12
B.	Agree	20
C.	Disagree	8
D.	Strongly Disagree	2
E.	Absent	2

He also had the students respond to the following: "I learned how to use the online catalog." The results were:

A.	Strongly Agree	21
B.	Agree	20
C.	Disagree	0
D.	Strongly Disagree	0
E.	Absent	3

By coding the remainder of the questions on the survey, Dan will be able to determine if these two questions were a good reflection of all of the lessons he presented, or if there were areas where the students did not feel as positive about the presentations. Dan will not be able to make any conclusions about the data until all of the responses have been tabulated and compared to the other two data sources used to triangulate the data. Through this process the action researcher is looking for patterns or themes. The action researcher should guard against making conclusions based on one data source. To preserve the reliability of the research, all three data sources must provide the researcher with the same answers to the questions.

Coding qualitative data will require more reflection on the themes which become apparent. While the researcher is examining the data she has collected, she should organize the data in piles as she determines different themes. Since qualitative data are the result of open-ended questions, the action researcher may have a more difficult time discovering these themes. If the researcher asks seventy people their opinion on the atmosphere in the library with an open-ended question, the library media specialist is likely to have seventy different answers. By reading all of the responses, the action researcher should find various themes and will then be able to divide the answers into like categories. If we look at the possible answers the library media specialist could receive with a question about the atmosphere in the library, the following would be typical responses. Question: "How would you describe the atmosphere of our library?"

- Pleasant
- Friendly
- Awesome
- Quiet
- I can't always find help when I come in.
- Fun
- Cold
- Okay
- The librarian is very busy.

The action researcher will need to determine what these answers mean. The "Friendly," "Pleasant," "Fun," and "Awesome" would be interpreted as positive responses. The "Cold" and "I can't always find help when I come in" could be categorized as negative responses. But what should the researcher do with "Quiet," "Okay," and "The librarian is very busy."? The researcher will need to add these to either the negative pile or the positive pile, or the researcher will need to see these as a different pattern and form a third category. The library media specialist certainly gains much information from qualitative data, but will need to spend more time reflecting on the data that are collected.

The library media specialist should treat the qualitative data collected through observations and journals in the same way. For example, after the students had received training in specific skills, Danielle observed how they demonstrated those skills during subsequent visits to the library. The following is her observation:

Observation Journal October 16th

Today's agenda consisted of passing out library cards, having the students check out books independently, and having them spend a bit of time perusing the online database for possible research topics. I watched a couple of students find their books. They went to the online catalog and spent about 10 minutes trying to find a title. Their keyboarding skills seemed to be deterring them from finding the needed information quickly. They then looked around to find the fiction section of the library and finally asked the library clerk for help. Then they retrieved their books without any problem. The whole process took about twenty minutes. Next I focused on two other students who were using the online database to explore possible research topics. These two young men were not as successful. They were able to quickly find the link on the home page, but it took them about five minutes to remember the first step they should take when they accessed the database. They finally asked for help, and I gave them a few clues and pointed out the poster identifying the steps to follow. Then they spent another fifteen minutes perusing the database.

After Danielle looks at all of her observational data, she will be able to see if there are any emerging patterns she can categorize. She will group similar occurrences together so she will be able to interpret her findings more easily after she has collected data from her three sources. After Danielle has sorted the qualitative data into like piles, she may assign point values to aid in having numeric values associated with the responses. For example, Danielle might tabulate her results: Students successfully finding their resources within ten minutes will have a value of five, while students who find their resources within 15 minutes will have a value of four. It is easier to use numbers instead of comments when comparing this data with the quantitative data she has already gathered.

Analysis of Data

After the library media specialist has administered all of the surveys, conducted all of the interviews, completed all of the observations, and reviewed all of the archival data, she is then ready to analyze and interpret her findings, an exciting part of the action research project. Now the researcher will begin to put the last pieces of the puzzle together to see what conclusions she can discover from the data that has been collected. The researcher should gather all of her data and determine what it is actually telling her. It is important to look at the original research question again and make certain that the collected data still "fits" with the question.

For example, Tom used a student survey, observations, and a teacher survey to see if the lessons presented in the library on how to use the online catalog were effective or not. He has the results coded from the three sources. Now he should combine the information gleaned from the three sources about the use of the online catalog into one report. From these three sources, Tom will be able to tell which lessons were effective and which were not. He will also find out if the lessons were more effective for some groups than for others. These results will help Tom plan the next steps in his project.

There are various methods to use in interpreting the data. Sagor gives detailed instructions on using a data matrix to interpret the results. In the matrix, Sagor has the themes the researcher has identified along the top of the matrix and the data sources along the side. The action researcher fills in the data in the appropriate boxes. This matrix gives the action researcher a visual representation of the collected data. (*Guiding*, *How*) Johnson explains how to use inductive analysis to interpret the data. The library media specialist should find the method she is comfortable with, codify the data, organize it, and interpret the answers to the initial research question.

Megan's Coding and Interpretation

Megan's research question: *How are students learning to be independent library learners through the new flexible schedule?*

Samples of Megan's coding:

Student survey
Question: How often do you ask to go to the library?
    Once a month 4   Once a week 25   Twice a month 8
    Twice a week 11   Almost every day 19

Question: Why do you come to the library?
    Because even though I can't read fast, I sometimes like to read.
    Because I like to read.
    Because I like books.
    So I can read more books to enjoy at home.
    Because I have to.
    Because I like to look at different books and mostly to look for a new book to read.
    Because my teacher makes me.
    To get books to learn to read better.

Observation of students
Megan gleaned the following from her observation of students.

Observation I: Upon arriving in the library the first thing the student does to find materials is:
    Go to the library staff. 16   Go to the computer. 54
    Go to the shelves. 33   Ask a friend. 1

Observation II: Students located material
    Independently 29   Required assistance 75

Survey of the school staff
Do you feel that the flexible schedule in the library is positively impacting student achievement?
    Yes 14   No 5

Why or why not?
- Yes, in part because I know I can be slotted in by simply looking at the schedule.
- The freedom of the flexible schedule allows the library media specialist to be available when needed.
- Not enough time to collaborate effectively.
- It's great to be able to let students go to the library whenever it is needed either in groups or as individuals.

Interpretation
The following results illustrate the information which Megan calculated after analyzing all of the data collected.

From the student surveys, I found that 49% of the 69 students were pleased with being able to come to the library whenever they needed to. From the student observations, I determined that 38% of the students were functioning independently when they came to the library. From the teacher's surveys, I discovered that only 45% of the teachers thought that the flexible schedule was impacting student achievement. In looking back at my question, "How are students becoming independent library learners through the new flexible schedule?" I realize that some of the data I have collected gives me a good snapshot of my situation. My first two sources, the surveys and my observations show that the students are becoming independent library users. The teachers' surveys are more subjective based on their perceptions of how the students have improved in the classroom since we implemented the flexible schedule. I need to work with the teachers and collect hard data as to the students' academic improvement before I can come to any definite conclusion about the effects of the flexible schedule on student achievement.

Chapter Summary

In Chapter 7 we discussed the methods to use in coding the data and interpreting the results. Both quantitative and qualitative data need to be organized into similar categories. The action researcher needs to tabulate the quantitative data and keep track of the comments gathered through the qualitative data. After all of the data is codified, the library media specialist must compare the data from each of her sources and develop logical conclusions. In analyzing the data, the researcher must make certain each data source is assessed. Addressing this triangulation of data will ensure the results of the study are valid and reliable.

8

Finalizing the Action Research

The library media specialist has reached a point where she needs to decide how to implement a plan of action. She has collected all of the data, analyzed this data, and now needs to decide what to do. The researcher has reached the point where she must devise a plan of action.

Spiraling Into the Future

As the library media specialist begins developing her plan of action, she should consider how her data collection has impacted the participants in her research. When a researcher conducts a survey, observes situations, or uses any other data collection techniques, negative and positive impacts may occur. The library media specialist should account for these occurrences in her plan of action. She should reflect on the following questions:

- Has my research project impacted the school community in a positive manner?
- Has there been any negative impact to the school community?

Answering these questions will give the library media specialist additional information to include in her overall action plan. The following comments were contained in Megan's reflection on the impact of her research.

> ### The Impact of Megan's Research
>
> *I feel that the action research project has had a positive effect on the Mountain Ridge Middle School staff. Several staff members have commented that the staff survey promoted conversations between teammates about how to incorporate the library and the library media specialist into upcoming units. I have noticed, as a result, that more teachers have been signing up for academic lessons in which I am able to incorporate the information literacy standards. I have also had the opportunity to collaborate in-depth with select teachers instead of "on the fly," the method of collaboration the previous librarian had employed. The research has given me confidence in knowing that many staff members support the changes I have made and are anxious to make the flexible schedule a success.*
>
> *I have noticed that there have been some negative impacts because of my research. A few teachers with negative views of the new library schedule have been given a platform to state their opinion through the staff survey. They may feel a confidence in having their thoughts made known and feel as though changes will be made according to their survey responses. The flexible schedule is new. I am learning how to use it along with the staff because it is new to me as well. Teachers may be quick to judge the schedule based on what they have seen so far. The principal and I have encouraged teachers who have mentioned going back to a fixed schedule to give it a year. They need to allow time for us all to stretch and grow into the new schedule and learn how to use the flexible schedule before deciding its success or failure. Continuing a flexible schedule for a year will also give me an opportunity to collect additional data especially in the area of student achievement. I need to work with the teachers and assess if the students have increased their academic achievement since we implemented the flexible schedule.*

After considering the negative and positive aspects of conducting the research, the action researcher must look at her total findings and ask a basic question: What steps should I follow to implement my findings? The purpose of developing a question, collecting the data, and interpreting the data is to arrive at this crossroad. Now the action researcher needs to decide whether to continue the course of action which was in place before the data was collected or to implement change. In some instances the action researcher will find that the procedures she was analyzing through her project are working well and there is no need to change. In Chapter 6 we saw how Nita and her team did not find any significant improvement in the performance of first graders who had attended an extended-day kindergarten. Based on this data, Nita and her team did not recommend that an extended-day program be implemented at their school. Their course of action should remain the same.

In many instances the data collected through the action research project will suggest that a change needs to occur. The library media specialist will then need to decide what to do. Mills presents a workable matrix that will help the action researcher outline where she is headed. Through this visual representation, the action researcher identifies her findings and lists the recommended actions, persons responsible for implementing the actions, and other entities to be contacted as the actions are being implemented. Mills also explains the timeline of implementation and resources needed to carry out the plan. Johnson suggests the action researcher list the conclusions and recommendations prior to developing the plan. Sagor suggests that the action researcher build a graphic reconstruction that addresses the pros and cons of all possible approaches to solving the problem. (*Guiding*)

The library media specialist may use any method she sees fit to develop her action plan. The critical element is that she takes her interpretation of the data and plans the next steps that should occur to implement her findings. The

58   Action Research: A Guide for Library Media Specialists

following examples illustrate action plans based on data that the library media specialists collected.

- The library media specialist found that feeder schools, current students and staff, and parents believed that computers with PC platform were best for their learning community and would assist the students in becoming lifelong learners. The library media specialist's plan recommended the school replace the Macintosh platform with the PC platform.

- The library media specialist determined through staff surveys, students surveys, and observations that a specific online database was the most effective source for students to use to complete their research. Her plan recommended that the meager library funds be funneled toward this specific source.

- The library media specialist determined through three methods of data collection that interacting with students in the library in their primary Spanish language contributed to the student's academic achievement. Her plan, therefore, supported interacting with these students as much as possible in their primary language.

- The library media specialist determined through the triangulation of sources that the teachers believed collaboration with the library media specialist would work only if portions of the allotted planning time were dedicated to collaborative planning. The library media specialist's plan recommended that the schedule be adjusted to allow for this type of planning.

- The library media specialist discovered that students, teachers, and parents were pleased with the partial flexible schedule she had implemented for student and staff access to the library. Her plan addressed expanding to a total flexible schedule at the beginning of the next school year.

Each of these examples illustrates how the action researcher has developed conclusions based on the data she collected and then made recommendations about what should be implemented in the future. This process is the essence of action research. As we have seen, the purpose of action research is reflective problem solving. Once conclusions are reached, then plans must be implemented to act upon these conclusions.

As the researcher is working on the implementation plan, she must determine the impact her recommendations will have on the entire school community. Once again, she should examine both the positive and the negative impacts of these recommendations. Now the researcher asks:

- What will happen if we implement this process?
- Will there be any negative impact on student achievement with this implementation?
- What will be the positive impact on student achievement because of this plan?

- Will the negative outweigh the positive impact?
- Will the positive outweigh the negative impact?

Answering these questions will guide the action researcher in proposing recommendations. The goal of action research is the improvement of one's program by increasing the academic achievement level of the students. If the improvement brings with it a myriad of problems which will impact the program in negative ways, then the action researcher will need to analyze these occurrences and determine if the program should be reevaluated before it is implemented. In other words, if the negative outweighs any positive results which will occur, then the recommendations should not be implemented as planned.

Sometimes the action researcher will not be aware of the potential negative impact until the plan has been implemented. Problems could occur that were not anticipated. The spiral of action research continues as an ongoing process. We have determined a problem, collected data, and implemented a solution. Now we need to reevaluate the solution we have implemented to make certain it is solving the original problem. As we reflect upon the plan we have implemented, we need to be aware of where we are in the improvement process. We may determine that we need to collect additional data, make other recommendations, and implement an additional plan. This is true action research; this is research to provide for constant and ongoing improvement for our professional practice. Look again at Figure 1.3. It illustrates the spiraling movement of action research. Action research is constant reflecting, analyzing, and implementing.

Megan used a matrix similar to the one suggested by Mills to determine her action plan. Her plan is illustrated in Figure 8.1.

Fig. 8.1. Megan's Plan. Adapted from Mills (126).

Summary of Findings	Recommended Action	Who is Responsible for the Action?	Who Needs to be Consulted or Informed?	Who Will Monitor or Collect Data?	Timeline
Students need more training in the online catalog	Schedule all sixth through eighth grade classes for retraining session	Library media Specialist and Classroom teachers	Classroom Teachers	Library Media Specialist	Retrain in September and conduct second observation in February
Teachers expressed a concern about the lack of time for collaboration	Library Media Specialist makes an effort to visit teachers during plan time on a regular basis	Library Media Specialist	Classroom Teachers	Library Media Specialist	Begin in September and conduct a second survey in December
Teachers are unsure how to use the Library Media Specialist and the basic procedures of the library	1. Staff training at September inservice 2. Compile a list of procedures and explain at the September inservice	Library Media Specialist	Principal and Classroom teachers	Library Media Specialist	1. September inservice 2. September inservice
Teachers are unaware of information literacy standards and confused about how they are to be taught	Explain information literacy standards at October inservice and show examples of lessons	Library Media Specialist	Principal and Classroom Teachers	Library Media Specialist	October inservice

Assessment of the Plan

The last step that the library media specialist must take before sharing her findings is the evaluation of the entire action research project. She must decide if this project affected student achievement in a positive manner. No project is perfect and the action researcher will realize that there are procedures that should be changed or data that should have been collected differently to enhance the value of the research. Maybe there is a question on the survey that the respondents did not understand. Perhaps the timeline could have been tweaked to provide fewer interruptions when the library media specialist was observing participants. Possibly the action researcher now feels she should have included more participants to collect more data. The possibilities are endless. No matter how detailed and reflective our plans are, we can always think of improvements to our project. As the library media specialist is planning how she will share her findings with other professionals, she must account for these possible improvements so she will be able to share this information.

> ## Megan's Assessment
>
> *I gained a tremendous amount of information through the process of this action research project. As a result I have been able to develop an action plan to improve the flexible schedule at Mountain Ridge Middle School to meet the needs of both students and staff as identified through the data collected.*
>
> *My research question was: "How are students learning to be independent library learners through the new flexible schedule?" I believe that the data proves that students are indeed moving in this direction. Both the teacher surveys and the student surveys supported the idea that students were becoming independent users. My observations of the student activity also supported this belief. The observations were not as productive as I had hoped because of a glitch in the cataloging function for the school district. On the days I was observing the students, the online catalog had corrupted data and the call numbers on the books did not include the first three letters of the author's last name. It was hard to evaluate whether the students really had the skills necessary to become independent learners in retrieving this material. Students may not have been successful in locating materials. However, my observations did show that many of the students were going to the computer first to locate materials. This told me that they were attempting to be independent instead of first going to a member of the library staff to find what they were looking for.*
>
> *A by-product of my research question provided me with information on the flexible schedule and its impact on student learning. I believe that the data collected showed that student learning is being impacted through the flexible schedule. Through the staff survey, I found that the majority of teachers believe that lessons created through thoughtful collaboration blend together classroom curriculum and information literacy standards. This collaboration impacts student learning more than lessons taught with the previous fixed schedule. Although the question asked on the student survey to collect data on this topic was weak, I still believe it shows that students are being impacted. Many lessons the students remember would not have been taught if the library had continued to operate on a fixed schedule. As stated earlier, I need to work with the teachers and collect hard data to document that student achievement has increased. Continuing my research to collect this data, will also allow me to continue observing the students as they come to the library and I can follow this observation with additional surveys or interviews.*
>
> *There are items I would have changed about this project. If I had continued this project over a longer period of time, I would have been able to retrieve more relevant data. If I were to conduct this research again, I would collect baseline data from the students and teachers at the beginning of the year before I introduced the flexible schedule. By comparing this baseline data with additional follow-up data, I would have results that I would consider more valid. Conducting the research over a longer period of time would allow the teachers and students to see more of the effects of how a flexible schedule impacts student learning. Although I regret not having the baseline data and a longer time to ease into the flexible schedule, I do feel that the data I collected gives me a snapshot of what we are like now and how we can improve in the future.*
>
> *Based upon the results of this study, I plan to revise my questions, still focusing on the students as independent learners through flexible scheduling. This will allow me to work more closely with the teachers and students through collaborative lessons while assessing the impact of a flexible schedule on student learning.*

Chapter Summary

In this chapter we discovered the necessity of examining our research methodology through both positive and negative lenses in the data collection phases and upon completion of the project. We also analyzed the data in terms of developing a plan of action which could be implemented to solve our original research problem. The final step in our action research plan is assessment of the project itself. Here the library media specialist analyzes portions of the study that need to be changed in order to collect more meaningful data. In this step the library media specialist must recognize potential problems and any negative impact that might occur due to her research. In the role of the action researcher she is now ready to share her findings with the professional learning community.

9
Sharing with Colleagues

The questions have been asked, the data collected and analyzed, the project has been evaluated, and a plan of action developed. Now the library media specialist is ready to share her findings with a variety of people. The three main avenues of sharing are with the school staff and district colleagues, at professional conferences through presentations, and by publishing the results of the research in professional journals. In this chapter we will look at each of these methods of sharing the action research results.

Before we look at "how" and "where" to share, we must address the "why" of sharing. Why should we share the information we have gained through our action research? The most obvious answer is that someone else can learn from what we have accomplished. That is a laudable reason but we are all very busy and, therefore, taking the time necessary to prepare sharing our results is just one more thing to add into our already busy day. Presenting the results of action research conducted for school improvement is actually our responsibility. We really do not have a choice. We are leaders in the library field and that leadership responsibility necessitates that we give back to our profession and provide guidance for others in the library arena. What better way to do that than through providing insight into specific aspects of our profession gleaned through our action research! *Information Power* encourages library media specialists to act as leaders in our profession both within the school and the learning community. The library media specialist should also model this leadership by being a member of the curriculum planning team. Our reflective practice for school improvement must be shared.

Sharing Locally

If the library media specialist has been working with a group of colleagues on the research project, then the initial sharing has already occurred. The library media specialist and the team should then present the findings to the principal or administrative team of the school. There are several ways to present this information and the action researcher needs to consider her own situation as she and her team prepare for this meeting. One way to facilitate sharing action research results is to give the administrators an overview of the process through an ongoing series of regular monthly meetings. The library media specialist can lay the groundwork as the project has developed. If an open environment has occurred throughout the project, then the meeting with the administration will be explained in the form of an update instead of a "new business" item. Whether it is an update or new information for the principal, the library media specialist should give an overview of the project and then provide the administration with the results of the data collection, interpretation of the data, and a synopsis of the recommended action plan. The library media specialist should discuss the reliability and validity of the project and share any concerns or problematic situations which occurred during the process. This meeting will be either formal or informal depending upon the relationship the library media specialist has with the administration. Through this discussion with the administration, plans should be made about how this information should be shared. The logical place to start would be with the staff at the school. The administration may also determine that the superintendent and school board in the district should receive these results. The principal should take the lead in paving the way for preparing an executive summary for the superintendent or the school board, requesting a meeting with the superintendent, or preparing a memo to be sent to the superintendent describing the background and the results of the research. The library media specialist and her team should focus on the staff presentation while providing the administrators with the necessary support if the administrators feel the research should be shared at a higher level.

Staff Presentation

In this initial meeting, plans should be made for sharing results of the action research with the staff at the school. If the action research project has school-wide implications, then the entire staff should be informed of the results and recommended actions. If the recommended actions will impact the entire staff, then the library media specialist must make certain that the presentation includes enough information to help the staff see the logical progression from research question, to data collection, to interpretation, and finally, to recommended actions. The library media specialist should present the following parts of the research project:

- Reason for the project
- Findings in professional literature
- Research question
- Triangulation matrix
- Data collection tools

- Data collection results
- Interpretation of the data
- Recommended plan of action

[Handwritten note: # compared to previous year]

In this presentation to the staff, it is not necessary to share the background information, as the staff will be aware of the school setting and learning community. The library media specialist may need to share statistics that directly relate to the reason for conducting the research. For example, if the school community has a school improvement goal of increasing the students' academic ability through use of a specific strategy and the project supports that strategy, then the library media specialist should share this information. In short, the library media specialist should make the presentation as relevant as possible to the staff and their teaching environment.

The library media specialist should use charts and graphs to illustrate her findings so that the staff will be able to process the information more easily. In conducting the research, the library media specialist has worked with students and staff on data collection and can relate the results in terms of this process. For example, the action researcher might say, "Remember the surveys you helped me with in the fourth and fifth grades? Well, here are the results." If the staff has been involved in this data collection, they will be interested in the findings. However, the library media specialist must be careful to honor the privacy and anonymity that she built into the data collection process. The presentation to the staff may be very formal or it may be informal depending on the atmosphere of the learning community. The action researcher must choose the best method of presenting this information and organize her presentation in this manner.

If the action research which the library media specialist conducted is not a school-wide project but one that is geared more to the function of the library media center, the library media specialist still needs to present the results of her research to the entire staff. Most changes that occur in the library will impact other members of the staff. The library media specialist must decide how much information is necessary to give the staff a good overview of the project and the implications it has for the academic achievement of their students. The presentation should include the same items as a school-wide project would include, but not with as much explanation. The library media specialist and her team should decide the most relevant aspects of the project and present this information to the staff.

District Presentation

Besides sharing the action research project with the library media specialist's staff, she should present the results of her research to her colleagues in the district. The other library media specialists in her district will be interested in the results of this project, especially if the action researcher has asked these colleagues to provide her with data. Each district is organized differently and the library media specialist should use the process appropriate to her district. If the district has a district-level coordinator of library services, the library media specialist should present the research to this person and request time at one of the scheduled meetings to present the action research results. For this presentation, the library media specialist should present the following portions of her project:

- Reason for the project
- Background information
- Findings in professional literature
- Research question
- Triangulation matrix
- Data collection tools
- Data collection results
- Interpretation of the data
- Recommended plan of action

For this presentation, the library media specialist should include the background of her school community because her colleagues may not know the specific statistics of her learning community. The library media specialist should highlight the data which she has collected from her colleagues since that information will be the most relevant to them. The library media specialist will need to work with the district coordinator on the time frame allotted for the sharing and adjust her presentation accordingly. It would be a good idea to present a "dress rehearsal" to the district coordinator so that she will be aware of the presentation information. This will allow the district coordinator the opportunity to reflect upon the research findings and determine the appropriateness for the district-wide program. This "dress rehearsal" will also allow the library media specialist to make certain her presentation is clear, appropriate, and relevant to the district program.

If the district does not have a district-level coordinator, then the library media specialist will need to be a bit more creative in sharing this information. She might share the information electronically with her colleagues, although this may be cumbersome as to the amount of information needing to be shared. Also, many library professionals are inundated with e-mails and may not have time to read and profit from the action research. A more effective way to share this information with her colleagues in other buildings may be to have an open house or an after-school get together either at the school, at her home, or local community center. In any of these settings, the library media specialist will be able to explain her reason for the research and the intricate parts of the project. This sharing is very appropriate to our roles as leaders in our profession. It also presents an opportunity to provide answers, suggestions, results, and possible solutions for problems that other library media specialists are experiencing in their own school communities.

If we look again at Megan's research, we see that her research is not an isolated situation appropriate only to her school. Many of our professional colleagues throughout the United States and other countries are analyzing the most effective way to promote student achievement through the library media center. Megan's research illustrates one method of increasing student achievement through the schedules implemented in the library media centers. A search in the professional journals using the terms "fixed" and "flex" will provide a plethora of information on the types of schedules in library media centers. Sharing our action research with professional colleagues may trigger an idea that they can use to explore their own school surroundings. This sharing will focus their reflection.

Sharing at Conferences

We have examined how the library media specialist should share her action research with her principal, the school staff, the superintendent, the school board, and the other library media specialists in her school district. This sharing should not stop at the boundaries of the school district. The action researcher should share her information at state and national conferences.

In presenting at either state or national conferences, the library media specialist needs to determine the format that will be the most appropriate for her presentation. There are a variety of presentation formats available at conferences. One commonly used format is a poster session. This is usually organized in a large area for a specific amount of time. Various presenters are located at tables throughout the room and conference attendees' progress randomly through the room, visiting with the presenters at each table. The poster session is very informal and allows for positive interactions between the presenters and the attendees. If the library media specialist determines that a more formal setting is more appropriate, then she should apply to present a session where she will be able to share her research. Here too, she will need to determine the type of session she desires to present. Some conferences allow for hour-long sessions, some for 45 minutes, and some offer pre-conferences which will involve a morning, afternoon, or an entire day of presentation. If the library media specialist wants to share the basic project and the results, then an hour or a 45-minute session is appropriate. If she wishes to provide some hands-on training on how to conduct action research, then a pre-conference workshop is more appropriate. Initially, the library media specialist will most likely choose an informal poster session or a timed session presentation.

When the library media specialist has determined the type of session she wants to present, then she should explore the possible conferences she believes will be the best to attend. The convention for her state association is a must. The action researcher must be aware that in order to present at the state conference, she will need to submit a proposal to the state conference committee about six months prior to the actual conference date. Depending on the size of the conference and the number of possible presenters, the library media specialist may or may not be selected to present. To increase the probability of being selected to present at the convention, the library media specialist must be very specific about the contents of her session. She should summarize her process, data, and findings as succinctly and clearly as possible. Conference committee members will be evaluating many proposals and are limited to selecting a certain number. The library media specialist must be able to convince the committee through her written words of the value of her session. One important aspect to consider is the intended audience. As we have seen, the purpose of action research is to increase student achievement through professional practice. The library media specialist needs to clearly state how her project supports student achievement through the instructional roles, information access roles, or management roles. Writing the initial application for a conference presentation is a necessary reflective process.

National conferences have a similar application process but the timeline is much different. Submissions for conference sessions are solicited a year or longer before the conference occurs. The library media specialist must submit an application which is relevant at the time of submission and also at the time the conference will take place. The focus of the application will be on the action research itself and on the spiral effect that the library media specialist has implemented. Explaining the implementation of the action plan will help the conference committee realize that the information will still be relevant at the time of the conference. They will not need to worry about the immediacy of the information.

Another consideration facing the action researcher is where to present. We have indicated that the library media specialist should present at her state professional organization and at national conferences. Initially, presentations should be given at conferences held by the organizations for our profession: the state library organization, the American Library Association (ALA) and the American Association of School Librarians (AASL), but these are not the only conventions the library media specialist should consider. The phrase, "preaching to the choir" describes what we often do in our profession. We present information to colleagues who already support our beliefs. Sharing our story is important especially if the results of our research will provide information that will improve student achievement in their learning community. We must share this information with other educational decision makers. Since our action research offers methods of improving academic achievement for students, then superintendents, principals, district administrators, and classroom teachers need to hear this information. The library media specialist should consider presenting at conferences for administrators, school boards, and for content areas of classroom teachers. Debbie in Chapter 4 conducted research on the effects of having the library media specialist implement technology into her daily schedule. She should share her findings not only with library media specialists but also with technology educators. In Chapter 5 Randy conducted research concerning the gifted-and-talented program in his school. He should share his findings with the gifted and talented educators since they too could profit from data he collected. Gary Hartzell in both editions of his book, *Building Influence for the School Librarian*, has encouraged those of us in the library profession to examine how we can share information about our profession with others. Sharing our research with our own professional colleagues is a must. But sharing this same information with others in the various ancillary areas of the field of education is also vital.

Conference presentations, whether state or national, can be intimidating to the library media specialist. We believe that we have valuable information to share but standing in front of a room full of our colleagues can be overwhelming. There are safeguards that a presenter can implement to be certain that the presentation will progress smoothly. The presenter should:

1. Locate the room prior to the presentation.
2. Bring one's own laptop for the presentation.
3. Bring a disc containing the presentation data.
4. Have a Plan B in case there is a problem with the technology. Plan B

could be bringing overhead transparencies to use if the LCD projector or computer malfunctions.
5   Check the availability of the Internet if it is needed for the presentation.
6   Bring screen shots of Web pages in case the Internet connection fails.
7   Check the layout of the room to ascertain that the tables and chairs are placed appropriately.
8   Check to make sure correct the number of handouts have been duplicated and are available for distribution.
9   Test the microphone to make sure it is working.

Following these tips will eliminate most common problems encountered with a presentation. Another problem that may occur is planning for a session of twenty participants and having only five show up or having 50 arrive. Either scenario presents challenges. If the number of attendees is small, the presenter may want to rearrange the room in a circle or semi-circle and present the information in an informal manner. Sitting in this fashion will allow for a more intimate setting and sharing will be free-flowing. If the numbers are much larger than anticipated, the presenter may run out of handouts and places to sit. The chair situation may not have a viable solution, but the presenter should distribute business cards so that participants can e-mail the presenter if they did not receive a handout. Another option is for the presenter to distribute a signup sheet if people did not receive handouts. The presenter will then be able to send the handouts electronically or via mail to the participants. Many conferences also post handouts on the conference Web site following the event.

A final tip for conference presentations is to remember that this public appearance is an opportunity for the library media specialist to share her action research with others. This sharing will further the profession and assist others in their quest for increased student achievement and educational excellence.

Publishing in Professional Journals

The library media specialist should also explore the possibility of preparing her work for a professional journal, another way to share authentic information with members of our profession. When discussing the possibility of publishing with a group of library media specialists, many times we are met with, "Oh, I don't write." Or, "I just don't have time." Or, "I don't really have anything to say." After conducting an action research project, the library media specialist has gathered enough data to be organized into an article. By following a few simple guidelines, publishing is really easy, fun, and professionally rewarding.

"Why should we publish?" University professors live with the phrase, "Publish or perish." Practitioners at the school level are not guided by this principle. Writing and publishing are ways we can give back to our profession.

When we present at a conference, we need a basic outline of what we are going to say. We then speak to our predetermined topics and answer questions from the audience. If we notice that the audience is confused or unclear about a statement we are making, we are able to clarify content at that time. We receive immediate feedback on the information we share.

When composing an article, the action researcher continues with the reflective process as she prepares the manuscript. She needs to employ certain mental gymnastics to make certain her ideas are clear, understandable, and valuable to those who will read the article. When the library media specialist publishes an article, this process allows her to share her research with many readers and does not limit her audience to conference attendees. The article also validates the research because the process of publishing includes working with an editor and reviewers to clarify points made in the article. The effects of presenting at a conference are limited, but the publication of an article allows this information to be shared through the indexing of the magazine. Those conducting research in the future will have access to what is printed today. Publishing will give the action researcher a sense of accomplishment when she shares ideas, thoughts, processes, and results with peers and professional colleagues.

The first step in writing is the hardest. That step is sitting down and putting ideas on paper. Many writers have rituals that they follow as they prepare to write. Some writers identify a certain time period during the day and use it exclusively for writing. Some writers hand-write their manuscript; other writers use a computer. Some writers have a designated work area established while others compose in a variety of locations. Many writers feel having established rituals is a necessary step to getting the creative juices to flow. After following any personal rituals, the writer simply needs to put words on paper. This is the first of many drafts and revisions so mechanics, specific words, and a variety of sentence structures can be adjusted later. The writer will spend quite a bit of time polishing the final product. Now the important step is to put ideas and thoughts on paper. Some writers work from an outline; others simply begin writing with a free flowing atmosphere to capture the ideas and then adjust later. The library media specialist needs to determine which method is best for her.

If the library media specialist is collaborating with a partner, the writers should determine the amount of time they will spend working on the project. They should have an overall timeline, a goal for when they will have a draft version of the finished project. They may want to allow a couple of weeks, a month, or an entire semester. The writers must understand that it is also important to have established timelines for each working session. Goals should be formulated for each meeting. The following questions will help the writers determine these goals.

- How many hours should we spend today?
- What is the best for our schedule?
- Which chapters will we work on?
- What have we accomplished since we last met?
- What goals do we want to accomplish today?

Whether the writing is a collaborative or solo project, the writer must determine the best time to write. Writing may be accomplished early in the morning or late at night, depending on our own internal clocks. In preparing this book, we decided that neither one of us was very lucid after a day at work and therefore, planned most of our writing sessions on the weekends. We found we were able to complete much more in a shorter amount of time by working with a weekend schedule.

Another consideration is if the library media specialist will write this by herself or if it is a collaborative project not only with a partner but also with her entire action research team. If the action researcher is collaborating with others, one method of conserving time is for one writer to put ideas on paper and then the group reacts, tears apart, starts over, or accepts the basic form of the work. If the team feels comfortable with writing the entire article together, that is certainly possible. Writers need to find the method that suits them the best. If the library media specialist is preparing the manuscript by herself, she would be wise to ask the staff members who were involved with the research to review the article to make sure it is focused, clear, and represents the research findings

The library media specialist must determine where she will publish the article. She should consider both journals from our profession and from organizations addressed by the content of the projects. After the library media specialist decides which journals are appropriate, she then determines the publishing criteria for that journal. For research in school libraries, the library media specialist should consider *School Library Journal*, *Library Journal*, *American Libraries*, *LMC: Library Media Connection*, *Library Media Activities Monthly,* and *Teacher Librarian*. Addresses for these publications are found in Appendix 1. Each journal has specific guidelines for submission of articles. Some journals accept manuscripts which are already prepared. Others require that the writer send a letter of inquiry to determine if the article will fit with the subject matter of the journal. Some organizations require an abstract prior to submitting the article. The criterion for each periodical is found at the beginning of the journal, usually close to the table of contents.

The library media specialist will also notice as she is exploring these different sources, that each periodical has different specifications for the article submission. Some of the considerations are:

- Length
- Type
- Margins
- Publication style form such as American Psychological Association (APA), Chicago Style, or Modern Language Association (MLA)
- Paper submissions
- Digital submissions
- Use of endnotes or footnotes
- Use of references or a standard bibliography

Another factor the library media specialist should consider is the matter of copyright. Some publications own the copyright of the material which is submitted, and some publications allow the author to retain the copyright. The library media specialist needs to be aware of these factors as she is determining where to submit her work.

Appendix 1 includes content-specific and administrative journals that the library media specialist should explore. Publications such as *Educational Leadership* published by the Association of Supervision and Curriculum Development (ASCD) should be considered as a possible venue. This publication prints materials intended for leaders at the elementary, middle, and high school levels. Action research projects relating to increased student achievement would fit well in this publication. There are endless possibilities of where the article might be submitted. The library media specialist must search for the journal which fits best with her subject matter.

After the library media specialist decides where to submit her research, she will need to follow the editorial guidelines for that periodical. The following sections are usually required in an article.

- Purpose of the study
- Background information
- Findings in professional literature
- Research question
- Triangulation of data
- Data collection tools
- Data collection results
- Data interpretation
- Succeeding interventions through the action plan

These are a few general guidelines that the library media specialist may encounter and will need to consider as she prepares to publish her research findings. Appendix 2 contains an action research project appropriate for publication. Even though writing requires considerable time and effort, the professional and personal rewards of publishing one's own work are well worth the effort.

Chapter Summary

In Chapter 9 we have explored sharing action research with other professionals. The library media specialist needs to share this information with the administration and staff of the school involved, as this information will affect their educational surroundings. The action researcher will then need to present this information to other district staff members. The library media specialist should consider presenting at state and national conferences. We examined various strategies to follow in preparing for each of these presentations. Finally, we looked at the reasons, processes, and guidelines for publishing an article in a professional journal. Researchers must share their findings in order to improve the professional practice of those of us in the field of education. We have all heard, "Don't reinvent the wheel." This adage applies to action research. If the library media specialist in one professional situation is concerned about a specific problem, it is likely that others share the same concerns or are looking for answers to the same or similar questions. Sharing is imperative.

A FINAL WORD

The authors could not write a book on action research for the library media specialist without a final word concerning the leadership role of the library professional. *Information Power* exhorts library media specialists to assume leadership roles in preparing their students for the twenty-first century. Library media specialists must also provide learning experiences and promote technology integration for their staff and the learning community.

In Chapter 1 we looked at action research as the reflective practice of problem solving for school improvement, student achievement, and accountability. This book has illustrated the process and methods to use action research for this purpose. In Chapters 8 and 9 we discussed the necessity of sharing action research with administrators, staff, and professional colleagues through presentations and publications. The role of the library media specialist does not stop with these activities. She must work collaboratively with the staff assisting them with using action research for improvement of their professional learning environment. The classroom teacher may not have the time to study the process of conducting action research. The library media specialist must guide the members of the staff in this process. The library media specialist should synthesize her knowledge of the process of action research and share these skills with the teachers. She may accomplish this through staff development workshops or working individually with teachers. Appendix 3 lists annotated Web resources the library media specialist may use to work with her staff. These resources are constantly changing, and the library media specialist should search for updated sites as she prepares to work with her staff. Some keywords that can be used to search for these sources are listed below:

- Action research
- Educational action research
- Informal education
- Library action research
- Teacher research
- Social sciences, methodology

Using these terms will provide the action researcher with a list of sites where she will find actual action research projects and the methods of conducting action research. The library media specialist will be able to select the most appropriate sources to use with her staff as they begin their action research process.

The action research journey is now complete, but the reflective problem solving of our profession will never end. Using the spiraling effect of action research, the library media specialist will continue to reflect and grow in her professional field. Sharing information with other colleagues will help the action researcher refine and internalize the process of reflective practice for professional improvement. Adding to the collective body of action research in the library field will energize both the library media specialist conducting research and colleagues sharing the research. Finally, the library media specialist will exercise her leadership responsibility in assisting others with the art of action research. The journey is just beginning.

APPENDIX 1

Contact Information for Journals

American Libraries
The Magazine of the American Library Association
50 E. Huron St.
Chicago, IL 60611
1-800-545-2433
americanlibraries@ala.org

American School Board Journal
1680 Duke Street
Alexandra, VA 22314
703-838-6722
submissions@asbj.com

Educational Leadership
Association for Supervision and Curriculum Development
1703 N. Beauregard St.
Alexandria VA 223311-1714
703-578-9600
el@ascd.org

Educational Technology
The magazine for managers of change in education
700 Palisade Avenue
Englewood Cliffs, NJ 07632-0564
201-871-4009 (fax)
EdTecPubs@aol.com

English Journal
Louann Reid, Editor, English Dept., CSU
1773 Campus Delivery
Fort Collins, CO 80523-1773
970-491-6417
English-Journal@ColoState.edu

Gifted Child Today
Resource for nurturing gifted and talented children
P. O. Box 97304
Waco, TX 76798

Independent School
The global schoolhouse
Editor, Independent School
NAIS
1620 L. Street, NW
Washington, D. C. 20036
202-973-9700
(10 pages or less)

JOPERD
Journal of Physical Education, Recreation & Dance
1900 Association Drive
Reston, VA 20191
703-476-3400
info@aahperd.org

Journal of the National Staff Development Council
Valerie von Frank
517-347-3006
NSCDValerie@aol.com
<www.nsdc.org/guides.htm>

Knowledge Quest
50 E. Huron St.
Chicago, IL 60611

LMC: Library Media Connection
Linworth Publishing, Inc.
480 E. Wilson Bridge Road, Suite L,
Worthington, OH 43085-2372

Mathematics Teacher
1906 Association Drive
Reston, VA 20191-1502
(See publication for requirements)

Mathematics Teaching in the Middle School
1906 Association Drive
Reston, VA 20191-1502
(See publication for requirements)

Middle School Journal
4151 Executive Parkway, Suite 300
Westerville, OH 43081
614-895-4730
howmanc@nmsa.org
<www.nmsa.org>

National Association of Secondary School Principals
1904 Association Drive
Reston, VA 20191
<www.principals.org/publications/bulletin/bulletin_guidelines.cfm>

Principal Leadership
<www.principals.org/publications/pdf/pl_guides.pdf>

Reading Teacher
International Reading Association
800 Barksdale Road
P.O. Box 8139
Newark, DE 19714-8139
<www.reading.org>

School Administrator
801 N. Quincy St., Suite 700
Arlington, VA 22203-1730
703-875-0772
magazine@aasa.org
<www.aasa.org/publications/sa/>

School Library Journal
360 Park Avenue South
New York, NY 10010
646-746-6759
slj@reedbusiness.com

School Library Activities Monthly
paulam@crinkles.com
(See publication for requirements)

Science Teacher
Manuscript Submission
1840 Wilson Blvd.
Arlington, VA 22201-3000
703-312-9239
tst@nsta.org

Social Studies and the Young Learner
Sherry L. Field, University of Texas-Austin
Dept. of Curriculum and Instruction
428 SZB, D5700
Austin, TX 78712-1294

Teacher Librarian
The Journal for School Library Professionals
Box 34069 Dept. 343
Seattle, WA 98124-1069
604-925-0266
admin@teacherlibrarian.com

Teaching Children Mathematics
1906 Association Drive
Reston, VA 20191-1502
703-620-9840. Ext. 2204
tcm@nctm.org

T.H.E. Journal
Technological Horizons in Education
ETC Group LLC
17501 17th Street, Suite 230
Tustin, CA 92780
(Unsolicited manuscripts become their property. Send inquiry first)

Young Children
Journal for the National Association for the Education of Young Children
<www.naeyc.org/resources/journal>

APPENDIX 2

Sample Project for Publication

The following action research project was conducted in an elementary school, employing the steps we discussed in Chapters 1-9. Not included in this sample, but included in the original body of work are graphs, charts, a triangulation matrix table, and a personal journal. Our purpose for including this project is to illustrate for the reader research that can be conducted at the school level and may be submitted for publication. We have identified the basic components that many publishers require for article submissions as noted in Chapter 9.

The Impact of Technology in the Library Media Center

By Julie Williams

(Purpose of the study: Julie sets the scene and explains the need for her action research.)

The Riverside Elementary School Library has gone through many changes over the past three years. With each modification, the library has improved. This year, Riverside Elementary School in the Colorado County School District (CCSD) has gone through a major alteration; it has combined two buildings into one. This consolidation meant that five rooms in the main building needed to become available for five classrooms moving from the second building. The computer lab room needed to be used as a classroom so the administration and the library media specialist decided to move the computer lab into the library. This affected the physical space of the library, naturally, but it has also affected the potential use of the library as well.

In addition to the physical changes in the library, this move has changed the responsibilities of the library media specialist. Last year, Riverside had a full time computer teacher. Because of budgetary constraints, the position of the computer teacher was eliminated beginning this school year. Thus, the library media specialist is expected to not only teach information literacy skills, but also teach technology skills. The new integrated block of study is called Information Literacy and Technology Skills.

On the surface, this seems like a positive move. It seems logical to have all of the information resources in one location. The questions, however, remain: How will moving the computer lab into the library impact the students' academic achievement? To what extent will the computer lab affect library instruction?

(Background information: Julie condensed the background section removing the personalized information.)

School Information: The Riverside Elementary School library serves a diverse group of students. Riverside Elementary School teaches Early Childhood Education (ECE), or pre-school, through fifth grade. Several years ago, Riverside was divided into two buildings because of high student enrollment. ECE through second grade was housed in the Primary Building and third through fifth grade was housed in the Intermediate Building. Last year, we were able to move first and second grades into the Intermediate Building. This year our student enrollment declined to about 350 students and we are now able to fit into one building.

Riverside was redesigned four years ago meaning that a new administrator and a new teaching staff were hired for that school year. This district-level decision was based on low test scores and behavior issues. The Colorado Student Assessment Program (CSAP) scores that year showed that only 21 percent of third grade students were at or above grade level in reading and only 18 percent of fourth grade students were at or above grade level in reading. Because the students were performing significantly below grade level in reading, Riverside adopted the Success For All Reading Program (SFA) at the time of redesign. SFA has proved to be effective at Riverside; more and more students are reading at grade level. The test scores have increased steadily since the redesign. Currently, 52 percent of third grade students, 21 percent of fourth grade students and 46 percent of fifth grade students are reading at or above grade level. During last year, Riverside received a "significant improvement" rating from Colorado's State Accountability Report and the Governor's Distinguished Improvement Award. With these honors, the state recognized that the scores of the Riverside students had increased dramatically over the past years.

Many of the teachers at Riverside are first year teachers or they are currently in the CCSD Teacher Training Program. Seventy-five percent of the staff have less than 10 years experience. Therefore, the new teachers do not have a wealth of resources in their own personal professional libraries. The professional resources they seek most are books about children of poverty and color, and books relating to special needs students. Reading, writing, and math are subjects that teachers feel comfortable teaching because we have school-wide programs for each; however, science and social studies are not outlined in school-wide programs. Teachers have also expressed an interest in trade books that illustrate reading comprehension strategies and writing techniques. They expect the library to provide them with print and electronic supplemental resources to facilitate their teaching.

At Riverside there is a heavy emphasis on standards-based instruction. Riverside teachers closely follow the curriculum matrix that the district has developed. Therefore, teachers generally stick to the topics outlined in their grade level's curriculum. The reading and writing blocks are regimented with a strict routine. Thus, teachers usually want to do library research projects that touch on other core subject areas, such as science, social studies, and technology.

Community Information: Riverside is one of 98 schools in the Colorado County Schools District. CCSD is an urban school system that services a diverse community. The neighborhood is predominately African-American and Hispanic. Sixty percent of the students who attend Riverside are African-American. Thirty-four percent are Hispanic. Three percent of the student population are Asian and the other 3 percent are Caucasian. The community surrounding Riverside is primarily low-income families with children. At Riverside, 89.6 percent of the students qualify for free or reduced priced lunch. Roughly 30 percent of the students we teach live with their extended family, and in some cases, in lieu of the nuclear family. Many students have neither quality reading materials nor computers at home and rely on the school library and the public library for these resources.

First and foremost, because our population is so diverse in culture, economic status, and beliefs, our collection and resources need to be diverse. I am new to the library field and just beginning my second year as the library media specialist at Riverside Elementary. Over the past year, I have been purchasing many books depicting the African-American and Hispanic populations. I see a need for both print and electronic resources in the library that support and advocate respect for diversity.

Library Information: Extensive weeding began two years ago and has continued in order to update the library materials. Prior to weeding, 40 percent of the collection was outdated (dating from the 1980s or earlier) or had inaccurate information. The collection was inventoried last year. As a result of weeding and conducting an accurate inventory, approximately 3,000 books were removed from the library. Because of this needed weeding, there are some major gaps in the collection, particularly in the technology, arts/leisure, and biography sections.

A few years ago, voters passed Mill Levy funding for CCSD libraries to improve their collections. The Mill Levy is divided among the schools based on need and student enrollment. Last year, the Riverside library received $2,000 from the Mill Levy fund. This money is in addition to the $2,000 allocated in the school budget. The district support and school administrative support greatly impacts Riverside's library collection. With this funding, we have been able to update our science, history, and geography collections. These newly updated areas are frequently circulating and are often used for research projects.

This year, the Riverside's library operates on a fixed schedule, meaning classes come to the library at a regularly scheduled time each week. This is a change from previous years. It was decided by the administration that the fixed library classes would provide classroom teachers with planning time. Last year, classroom teachers had three 50-minute blocks of planning each week due to the music class, the gym class, and the computer class. This year, teachers are still allocated three 50-minute blocks of planning each week except that instead of a computer class, students attend the Information Literacy and Technology Skills class.

The current administration has been very supportive and has made improving the library a priority at Riverside Elementary. Our vision is to have the library fully updated in terms of resources and appearance. In addition, it is our goal that the library becomes fully functional for students, teachers, staff, and community members. In order to accomplish this goal and include the technology component with the library media specialist's job description, I need to determine if others have tried this configuration. Therefore, I need to conduct a thorough review of the current literature in the field.

(Findings in the professional literature: As Julie searched the literature, she found solid sources to provide a context for her research.)

Because adding technology to libraries and library instruction is a recent issue across the nation, much has already been explored on this topic. Many articles investigate how technology and computer labs impact school library instruction and student achievement. This concern is so widespread that prominent publications such as *School Library Journal* and *Teacher Library Media Specialist* have featured articles that discuss this issue in depth. Many sources covering this topic can be found by searching through the online journal databases. The Internet, as well, serves as an adequate resource for articles that discuss technology in library media centers.

Most articles discussed that the use of technology in school library media centers would have a positive impact on student achievement. Several sources also pointed out that it would add significant preparation and instructional time to the library media specialist's workload.

Many articles expressed that the use of technology in library instruction positively impacts student academic achievement. Farmer's article, "Getting an Early Start on Using Technology for Research," speaks to the importance of integrating information literacy skills with technology skills. One way to achieve those skills is to have students conduct research using the technology available in the library. For example, if students were to use the Internet to find reliable and accurate information, they are practicing critical thinking skills, skimming and scanning skills, computer skills, and compare and contrast skills. The process of using computers will help students become *savvy information researchers* by practicing and mastering these skills.

The article "Library Technology Raises Test Scores, Too" which appeared in *School Library Journal* also examines the impact a well-equipped library has on student academic achievement. Minkel, the editor, refers to the Keith Lance Colorado study that states when students have access to online databases and high quality computer resources, they achieve higher test scores on standardized tests. Students who work with library media specialists and are taught how to actively locate and use information on the Web gain basic information literacy skills which they need in order to do well on these standardized tests.

In order for technology to positively impact student academic achievement, it is essential to create meaningful and authentic learning experiences with technology and information literacy skills. Champlin and Loertscher, in the article "Reinvent Your School's Library and Watch Student Academic Achievement Increase," provide four techniques for achieving a technologically effective library media center through collaboration. One essential factor is for the principal to be very supportive and encourage the library media specialist and teachers to use the print and electronic materials in the library often. The authors also stresses the importance of collaboration between teachers and the library media specialist, creating meaningful, authentic units of instruction that integrate technology skills into the information literacy skills. To achieve success, however, the library media specialist needs to be highly qualified, technology savvy, and devoted to the needs of the library on a full-time basis.

Learning and Leading with Technology magazine featured an interesting article written by two fourth grade students, Blum and D'Ignazio, at Apex Elementary School in Apex, North Carolina. The article "After the Internet ... the Encyclopedia?" examines what students learn from using technology in the research process. The two fourth grade students expressed that they benefited greatly from the technology they used, primarily CD-ROM's and Internet resources. These students were able to retain content knowledge about the solar system and gained technology skills by participating in the research process.

According to the previously listed articles, having access to technology in the library is a beneficial resource to students in their quest for academic success. This integration, however, does not lighten the library media specialist's workload. With this background of the literature in mind, it was time to clarify my thoughts and develop questions for possible research.

(Research questions)

For this project, I explored the following questions. First, I wondered, "how will moving the computer lab into the library impact the students' academic achievement?" Overall, this is the most important question. Everything we do in education should be intentional. Moving the computer lab into the library to save space seemed to be a last minute decision. Therefore, we really need to examine the effects this move will have on instruction and student achievement.

Next, "to what extent, if any, will the computer lab impact library instruction?" It seems having many computers in the library will enhance library instruction. Computers and access to the Internet provide more resources to the library. The question is to what extent do the benefits of having 30 computers outweigh the constraints on the physical space and the library media specialist's instructional time?

Finally, "what additional responsibilities will having the computers in the library add to the role of the library media specialist?" This is also very important to consider. Changing from a flexible schedule to a fixed schedule really cuts down on the amount of time each class can spend in the library each week. Therefore, the library media specialist will need to be creative about integrating technology skills with information literacy skills. Will this add another level to the library media specialist's very full plate?

(Triangulation, data collection and interpretation: Julie combined this information in the following section.)

Most articles presented above caused me to believe, in general, the computer lab would have a positive effect on student achievement, yet it would add significant preparation and instructional time to my workload. Each situation is different; thus I needed to explore how exactly this change would affect Riverside Elementary School. In order to investigate how the computer lab would impact student achievement and affect library instruction at Riverside Elementary, I needed to collect and analyze many sources of data. I developed a triangulation matrix in which I surveyed students, questioned teachers, collected assessment test data, and noted observations in a journal.

Riverside Elementary School teachers use step-by-step district approved curriculum with every lesson. At the time that Riverside was redesigned, student achievement was very low. In order to increase student achievement, it became imperative for all lessons, including those lessons taught in the library, to be connected to the state and district standards in order to positively impact student achievement. This leads to the most important question: How will moving the computer lab into the library impact the students' academic achievement? I collected several sources of data to explore this question.

Student Pre-Survey: At the beginning of this action research, third, fourth, and fifth grade students were surveyed to determine their attitudes and to assess what they already knew about library and technology skills. These students were selected because they have had many experiences using the computer lab and library in years past. Ninety-seven surveys were collected during the first weeks of school.

The first question on the Student Pre-Survey asked, "Why do you come to the library?" Student perception of the library overwhelmingly showed that students believe the library to be a place to "check out books." Forty-nine students said they come to the library to "check out books" and 39 students said they come to the library "to read." This information seems to indicate that the majority of students do not consider the library to be a place to research and learn from a variety of sources, such as print and electronic materials. This makes sense because in past years there were a limited number of computers in the library and they were generally used to search for books using the library automation system, District Online Catalog (DOC). Also, in years past, students primarily came to the library to check out books for reading pleasure, not for research. Other responses to the survey included 11 students recognizing the library as a place "to learn," four students "like to look at books," three students "use the computers," and two students identified each of the following three activities: "conduct research," "learn library skills," and "read for the Million Words Campaign." One student said she comes to the library "to play on the computers" and one comes "to have fun."

The pre-survey also examined how the computer lab was used when it was a separate class and disconnected from the library. Although it appears that some classes used the computers to supplement resources for research projects, the majority of students used the computer lab to play games and explore the Internet for entertainment purposes. Student were asked the question, "What kinds of things did you learn in the computer lab last year?" Twenty-five of the students responded that they learned how to use Internet games and 11 students responded that they learned how to play computer games. That is nearly one-third of the students surveyed. It appeared that only eight students used the computers for academic information and information literacy skills.

When asked to specify how often students used the computer for academic versus entertainment purposes, 45 of the students responded they used the computer for computer games most of the time. It appears that students used technology in years past for entertainment more often than for academic purposes.

When asked to respond to how well students know how to use specific computer programs as a result of the previous year's instruction, 67 of the students responded that they knew how to operate a computer drawing program and game programs. Sixty-one students responded they "really knew how to use" computer game programs. Therefore, because the computer lab was independent of library instruction, students had not learned that the computers could be a useful resource for information access and production. Interestingly, the students overwhelmingly expressed that the computers helped them learn in the previous year, even though they also expressed that they rarely used the computers for educational purposes. Sixty students responded that the computers helped them learn "a lot" last year. This data shows that the students perhaps are highly motivated by the computers and increased their computer technology skills, even though they did not seem to learn academic content by using the computers.

Student Post-Survey: To evaluate if students benefited from technology used in the library this year, a Student Post-Survey was given to the same 97 students three months into the school year. During these three months students received instruction on how to access information through the use of online research databases. Most students seemed to learn that the computers are a valuable resource for learning information. It is particularly encouraging that students expressed that the computers helped them learn district required standards and content. Forty-four students expressed that they learned research skills by using the computers and only one student expressed she learned how to play games on the computer this year. This data will help determine whether or not the computers can have a positive impact on student academic achievement. Further investigations will need to take place over the school year to determine whether or not students are actually retaining learning standards and content information through using computers.

Overall, students expressed that so far this year the computers have helped them learn. All classes in third through fifth grades used the Internet and online databases to gather information for their research reports. When asked specifically what computer programs helped them learn this year, 60 students responded that the online research programs helped them more than any other technology resource. The students seem to be benefiting from the added technology and the integrated information literacy and technology instruction.

CSAP Data: In order to assess that students are really benefiting from the computer lab in the library, it is necessary to also look at how they perform on assessments that evaluate their information literacy skills. In an article edited by Minkel, "Library Technology Raises Test Scores, Too," Keith Lance, the Director of Library Research Services, states that students achieve higher scores when they can locate, evaluate, and use the information accessible through the World Wide Web. When students are using the computer to explore information, they are using the same skills they will need to use on assessment tests. They need to know how to skim and scan a text, locate information, make sense of the information, and use the information in a meaningful and comprehensive way. The Colorado Student Assessment Program (CSAP) assesses the proficiency of third through tenth grade students in their information literacy skills.

The most current CSAP results show that fourth grade students at Riverside are in dire need of instruction in information literacy. Only 27 percent of the students were able to demonstrate proficiency in this area. Likewise, only 50 percent of all fifth grade students were proficient. As the student surveys revealed, students received minimal information literacy instruction during this past school year, particularly during their library and computer classes. These test results confirm that Riverside students critically need instruction in information literacy through technology integration. Throughout this year, students will receive more opportunities to develop these skills during their Information Literacy and Technology Skills block. Because there will be an increased emphasis on technology in the library instruction, it will be interesting to see if students are able to increase their information literacy skills through the integration of technology. Using this information as baseline data and comparing it with the next CSAP results will give a clearer picture as to whether this instruction is positively impacting student achievement.

Teacher Questionnaire: Using my third means of data collection for my triangulation matrix, to further examine how students' academic achievement will be impacted by technology instruction, I surveyed the classroom teachers who are constantly assessing the success of their students on different state standards. Therefore, they are able to see if students are benefiting from information literacy and technology instruction. Through email, the classroom teaching staff was given a Teacher Questionnaire. Out of the 15 classroom teachers on staff, 10 responded to the email.

Teachers were asked, "How will student achievement be impacted by the computer lab being used in the library." Two first grade teachers responded that they did not believe that the computer lab being used in the library would impact student achievement. These teachers believe that at such a young age, first grade students are not developmentally ready to benefit from the computers. They expressed that basic reading skills would need to be in place first before students could gain academic benefits from technology. Seventy-five percent of the responding teachers believed that it would have a positive impact on student achievement. Some of the following comments were included:

Having technology instruction in the library would:

- Help students understand technology as a resource or tool rather than a source of entertainment.
- Enhance content instruction.
- Motivate students to learn content material.
- Help bridge a connection between technology, research, and library.

Teachers were also asked "Do you think moving the computer lab into the library was a positive change or a negative change? Why?" All of the teachers responded that they thought the change was a positive change. Ninety percent of the teachers expressed that the computer lab had the potential to supplement the resources in the library and enhance library instruction.

When asked, "What are the benefits to library/technology instruction?" seventy-five percent of the teachers saw it as a way to connect literacy to technology skills. Sixty-seven percent of the teachers also saw that the computer lab could help integrate research standards and technology standards, both required by the district.

Based on the information provided by teachers, using the computer lab during information literacy instruction has the potential to augment instruction, whether or not student achievement would be impacted. Teachers seemed to be ambivalent as to whether technology instruction would impact student achievement. This survey asked the teachers what their opinions were but their answers were not based on actual data. Teachers will provide hard data at the end of the year based on CCSD assessments.

How will moving the computer lab into the library impact the students' academic achievement? The findings of the above data seem to point to a positive result. Based on the opinions of students and teachers, the computer lab has the potential to positively impact student academic achievement. The results, however, are incomplete. Student achievement in information literacy skills will need to be monitored throughout this school year by assessing student work, creating classroom evaluations, and analyzing standardized tests, such as the CSAP.

Although it appears that the computer lab may positively affect student achievement, I also need to examine how the computer lab will affect library instruction. This school year is a transitional year for the library media center. Not only has the computer lab been moved into the library, the library is also moving from a flexible schedule to a primarily fixed or permanent schedule. Because of these changes, it is necessary to examine how much of an impact adding technology to the information literacy instruction will be for my position. Champlin and Loertscher, in *Principal Leadership Magazine*, express that in order for students to build information literacy skills, the library needs to be staffed by a powerful learning and technology literate school library media specialist. As the library media specialist, I need to be an expert in resources and a provider of meaningful learning experiences. Now that the computer lab is in the library, I also need to become familiar with all of the resources that technology can provide. This will impact the amount of planning time I use to investigate and evaluate the electronic resources in the library.

Student Pre and Post Surveys: At the beginning of the year, I needed to survey the students in order to know what skills I should teach during their Information Literacy and Technology class. As stated above, the Student Pre-Survey revealed that students did not recognize the library as a place to learn research and technology skills. At the beginning of the year, only ten percent of the 97 third, fourth, and fifth grade students surveyed said they come to the library to learn information and conduct research. I must change this perception by providing meaningful learning experiences for these students, through the integration of information literacy and technology instruction.

In addition, students conveyed that they had little experience using the computers in an educational way. Last year, students were not consistently exposed to publishing programs (word processing and presentation) and they were not consistently exposed to online database resources as a source of information. Therefore, now that I am primarily responsible for teaching technology skills, I am responsible for researching effective ways to incorporate the computers into information literacy lessons. After three months of integrated instruction in which students were learning content, research skills, and technology skills, 70 percent of the students said that now they are using computers to help them learn.

Journaling: After reviewing my journal from the past three months, it is apparent that information literacy instruction has been enhanced by the technology component. The technology component, however, has also increased preparation and planning time and it has prolonged time spent on student projects.

Each week I was averaging between two to four hours researching electronic resources. Often, I found that the information on the Internet and online databases was not age appropriate for elementary students. It was difficult to find Web sites that were both user-friendly and written at the appropriate reading level. Because of this issue, I needed to create Web Quests to help students make sense of the information they were using from these electronic resources.

I also spent much of my planning time anticipating problems the students would encounter as they navigated the Internet and online database resources. I needed to provide computer mini-lessons in which I reviewed basic navigation skills (such as pointing with the mouse cursor and clicking the mouse button). I observed that students were much more savvy using the computers as a publishing tool than as an information resource. This assisted in the planning process; I was able to use print materials that were appropriate for the students, yet integrate the computers into the publishing portion of the research process. The time spent preparing and planning these technology lessons decreased as the school year progressed. As students became more familiar with basic research skills and as I became more aware of what to look for, I found myself spending less time in preparing these lessons.

Instructional time with students was also affected by the integration of the computers into the library. Several times over the past few months, unforeseen problems occurred and instructional time was affected. For example, when the fifth grade students all tried to search the online encyclopedia at the same time, it slowed the network system down so that the Internet was very slow in responding to commands. This affected instructional time and prolonged the completion of student projects. In order to combat some of these unforeseen issues, I found that instructing students in small groups was very effective. Simpson, in the article "Information Technology Planning" discusses that the most effective way to instruct students in technology skills is in small groups. Based on Simpson's research, instructional groups should be comprised of two students for primary levels, three for elementary, and four with middle and high school levels. Not only do students benefit from the small group instruction because they receive more individual attention, using small groups also relieved the overload on the school's infrastructure.

Teacher Questionnaire: Elementary school teachers are often overwhelmed by the amount of material that should be covered each school year. In fact, it is extremely difficult for the classroom teachers to teach all of the standards and content required in one year. Because of this issue, it is important for the classroom teachers to collaborate with a highly skilled library media specialist.

Teachers were asked in a Teacher Questionnaire, "Are there standards/subjects you are unable to cover in depth during your instructional block?" Thirty percent of the teachers admitted that they had difficulty covering technology standards, social studies standards, and science standards. Each of these areas can be addressed through collaboration with the classroom teachers during the Information Literacy and Technology Block. In years past, teachers relied on the computer teacher to cover basic computer skills and the district's technology standards. Now that the computer teacher has been eliminated and technology instruction is integrated with information literacy standards, teachers are relying on the library media specialist to provide instruction in these areas. Sixty percent of teachers are willing to collaborate with the library media specialist in the areas of social studies and science. Based on this data, the lessons in the library need to integrate technology and information literacy as well as incorporate social studies and science content. Champlin and Loertscher suggest that if teachers are overwhelmed by technology or the school does not have enough equipment for the classrooms, establishing a library learning laboratory makes sense. Teachers at Riverside Elementary are overwhelmed by the amount of content and skills they need to cover within one year. This creates a definite need for teachers to collaborate with me on information literacy and technology projects.

(Action plan: Julie analyzed the impact of the research and provides plans for continuing the spiral of action research.)

This research project has positively impacted Riverside's library. I anticipated that moving the computer lab into the library would create positive changes in student achievement and library instruction. The data thus far shows that integrating technology into the lessons of the library has the potential to contribute to the academic success of our students. For years teachers have complained that computer time was wasted instructional time. Teachers felt that their students were just playing games and not gaining any academic benefits. This project provided a framework to assess just how effective integrating technology into library skills instruction can be. Further data will need to be collected to determine precisely how much of a positive impact the integrated Information Literacy and Technology Block will be on student achievement.

This action research also revealed that adequate time will need to be allotted to planning and creating integrated learning experiences. At the beginning of this research process, I anticipated that adding the computer lab to the library would impact the amount of time I could devote to planning and instruction. For instance, I realized that I would need to devote time to researching effective ways to integrate technology into the information literacy class. My research indicated that the amount of time was considerable at the beginning of the year, yet as time progressed, less time was needed in the planning and preparation of technology integration lessons. I also anticipated that instructional time would be impacted by the integration. For example, instructional time would need to be devoted to teaching basic computer skills so that students could use the computers during their research projects. Again, the research indicated that considerable time was necessary to teach these skills at the beginning of the school year, but as the school year progressed, less time was needed during instructional time for basic computer skills.

As the data above indicates, continuing the integration of technology skills is beneficial. I will, however, need to collect more data and assess how student achievement is being impacted and how the information literacy instruction is being affected. For instance, I will not have the current CSAP results until next summer, so I will need to wait for these results to determine whether or not the integrated instruction was effective. In addition, each year I will need to assess how the computer lab can best be used in the instruction of information literacy. I will need to assess whether or not my instruction is beneficial to the students' academic achievement each year using district and teacher data. This research could also be beneficial with our school's pursuit of additional funding through grants. If the computer lab proves effective, than it may help in our pursuit of technology funding or extra paraprofessional staffing in the library media center. Since I lost the flexible schedule in the library, I need to determine if the benefits of integrating technology into the library through the implementation of a fixed schedule is impacting the students' academic achievement.

(Conclusion)

Examining the impact of technology in the library media center was a valuable project. This action research has created a framework from which I can assess the impact of integrating technology with information literacy. I was able to begin assessing student achievement and examine how best to provide integrated instruction. I now have the tools necessary to collect data and analyze that data. I have also become a resource for my school in terms of conducting action research. I am able to assist other teachers in exploring this process of analysis and reflection.

One of the most valuable aspects of this project was the journaling component. However, it was the most difficult factor in completing this project. Lack of time is always an issue in education, especially elementary education. Finding the time to reflect on my teaching and its impact on student growth was difficult. From the journaling I gained significant insight into the effectiveness of my teaching and planning. As a result, I plan to write in a journal regularly in order to provide the best instruction for my students.

This particular action research project will continue over the next few years. The information gathered from this project so far has been a valuable resource both to me as the library media specialist and our school in planning for the future. I anticipate that the research will continue to produce indispensable insights.

(Works Cited)

Blum, Ashley, and Laura D'Ignazio. "After the Internet...the Encyclopedia?" *Learning & Leading With Technology*, May 1999: 54-57.

Champlin, Carol, and David Loertscher. "Reinvent Your School's Library and Watch Student Academic Achievement Increase," *Principal Leadership. Middle School Ed.*, Mar. 2003: 67-70.

Farmer, Lesley S. J. "Getting an Early Start on Using Technology for Research." *Library Talk*, Mar./Apr. 2002: 24-26.

Minkel, Walter, Ed. "Library Technology Raises Test Scores, Too," *School Library Journal*, Dec. 2002: 24-26.

Simpson, Carol Mann. "Information Technology Planning: Computers in the School Library – How Many Are Enough?" *Knowledge Quest*, Sept./Oct. 2002: 23-26.

This sample illustrates how Julie Williams was able to condense her research findings into a possible article for publication. Her project shows how she used action research skills to identify a problem affecting her school library and determine a course of action to follow to increase student achievement. As noted in her conclusion, she is using the spiral of action research to continue with her professional improvement.

APPENDIX 3

Web Resources for Action Research

Baker, W. *Action Research for Teachers by Teachers.* Spring 2000. University of North Carolina at Pembroke. <www.uncp.edu/home/baker/actionresearch/>. University faculty developed this action research Web site. It includes many useful articles and links to concrete applications and an understanding of the topic.

Brown, Mary. *Action Research.* 1 May 2003. University of Southern Connecticut. <www.southernct.edu/~brownm/act1.html>. The Department of Library Science and Instructional Technology at the University of Southern Connecticut at this resource present supplementary materials for the study of action research. This source provides a step-by-step explanation of the process of action research.

Cornell Participatory Action Research Network at Cornell University. 2004. PARnet. <www.parnet.org/>. Known as the oldest action research Web site in the world, PARnet sponsors this internationally known resource. It is unique as it offers online participation, local activities calendar, and postings of current articles and information on the topic.

Delong, Jackie, Cheryl Black, and Heather Knill-Griesser, Ed. *Action Research in Grand Erie.* 2003. Grand Erie District School Board. <www.actionresearch.ca>. The projects and research papers by teachers and administrators of the Grand Erie School District in Ontario, Canada are shared to encourage evidenced based practice and the further use of action research in the K-12 educational arena.

Dick, Bob. *Action Research Resources*. 22 Apr. 2003. Southern Cross University. <www.uq.net.au/action_research>.
> The links, articles, and other resources available on this Web site are part of a 14-week course entitled Action Research Online (Aerol) offered by Southern Cross University, New South Wales, Australia. The Action Research course may be taken via the Web and email.

Disney Learning Partnership. *Action Research for School Improvement*. Date unknown. Disney Online. <http://disney.go.com/disneylearning>.
> This Web site offers a simple explanation of the action research process and its focus on student achievements by searching on the term "action research."

ALTEC. *Action Research Network*. 2003. University of Kansas. <http://actionresearch.altec.org/>.
> This Web site, developed by the Advanced Learning Technology (ALTEC) department of the University of Kansas provides students and professors with an opportunity to share their current and ongoing research. The free Web site offers a login option for peer editing of research projects.

Hatten, R. Donna Knapp, and Ruth Salonga. *Action Research: Comparison with the Concepts of 'The Reflective Practioner' and 'Quality Assurance'*. 24 Aug. 1999. University of Sidney. <www.scu.edu.au/schools/gcm/ar/arr/arow/rdr.html>.
> This Web site was developed to explain the differences and similarities between the reflective practitioner, quality assurance, and action research methodologies by three Australian graduate students.

Lamb, Annette. *Information Based Inquiry for Teachers*. Jan. 2004. Annette Lamb and Larry Johnson. <http://eduscapes.com/info/achievement.html>.
> Dr. Annette Lamb developed this course for Indiana University to assist teachers with their understanding of action research. Her page of evidence-based programs and practices is especially useful to school library media specialists when looking at quality programs and student achievement.

Mettetal, Gwynn. *Classroom Action Research Overview*. Date unknown. Indiana University, South Bend. <http://mypage.iusb.edu/~gmetteta/Classroom_Action_Research.html>.
> Gwynn Mettetal developed this Web site at Indiana University to assist teachers with the action research process. She explains the differences between action research and formal research. Dr. Mettetal outlines the steps needed to conduct action research, offers resources, and lists some Indiana initiatives.

Newman, Judith. *Action Research: Exploring the Tensions of Teaching*. 2003. Lupinworks. <www.lupinworks.com/ar/>.
Dr. Judith Newman designed this Web site to connect teachers to the action research process. A reflective look at teaching, links to other action research Web sites, the *English Quarterly*, and the author's action research articles are included in this resource.

NPower Online Survey Tools. 2004. Npower National Network. <www.npower.org/tools/guide+to+online+survey+tools.pdf>.
Npower is a national network of non-profit institutions sharing technological innovations. This is a published report that compares electronic survey tools.

Painter, Diane and Leo Rigsby. *Teacher Research: Action Research*. 13 Nov. 2003. George Manson University. <www.gse.gmu.edu/research/tr/TRaction.shtml>.
The Graduate School of Education at George Manson University offers this extensive Web site which includes the history of action research, related Web links, and a Power Point on the topic.

Parsons, Sharon. *Teacher Research*. 2003. San Jose University. <www.accessexcellence.org/21st/TL/AR/>.
This Web site at San Jose University was developed to show the steps needed to conduct action research for teachers. Links to online resources, discussions, and action research examples are included in the content.

Pendergast, Michael. *Seven Stages in my First Action Research Project*. 1994. Queen's University. <http://educ.queensu.ca/projects/action_research/michael.htm>.
This Queen's University Web site hosts Michael Pendergast's journal of impressions as he steps into and through the door of action research as an M.Ed student. His project is to relate the attitudes of his second grade students to reading and writing and their levels of confidence in their abilities.

Richardson, Joan. *Teacher Research Leads to Learning, Action*. Feb./Mar. 2000. National Staff Development Council. <www.nsdc.org/members/tools/t-feb00.pdf>.
Download this file to use this publication by the National Staff Development Council to walk a teacher group through the step-by-step process of action research. Directions, notes, and facilitator instructions are furnished with this pre-designed teacher inservice packet.

Ryder, Martin. *Action Research in Education*. 1 July 2004. University of Colorado at Denver. <http://carbon.cudenver.edu/~mryder/itc/act_res.html>.
Dr. Martin Ryder has assembled a vast variety of links to up-to-date definitions, journals, and numerous references on action research. This Web site provides extensive knowledge to anyone interested in the topic.

Smith, Mark. *Action Research: A Guide to Reading*. 14 July 2002. Infed. <www.infed.org/research/b-actres.htm>.
This Infed (non-profit organization) sponsored Web site offers information on action research including an introduction, the origins, its history, the process, and further readings.

Taylor, M. *Action Research in Workplace Education: A Handbook for Literacy Instructors*. Jan. 2002. National Literacy Secretariat of Canada. <www.nald.ca/CLR/action/cover.htm>.
The National Literacy Secretariat of Canada has developed this handbook on action research to assist with change in literacy practices in teaching and learning. The Web Site contains background information, examples, and templates for the action researcher to use in developing her own project.

University of Cambridge Faculty of Education. ARTE International Project. *Action Research in Teacher Education: Investigating the Personal and Social Dimensions of Teaching and Learning*. 2004. University of Cambridge. <www.educ.cam.ac.uk/arte/index.html>.
This Web site was developed as part of a conference and partnership project between the University of Cambridge Faculty of Education and three secondary schools in East Anglia, England. These groups as well as teachers from Holland, the USA, and Russia shared educational applications of action research. Contact information on the participants is provided for the ongoing project.

Wilson, Brent. *Welcome to Research in ILT*. 2 May 2004. University of Colorado at Denver. <http://thunder1.cudenver.edu/ilt/it_6720/wilson/index.htm>.
Dr. Brent Wilson of the University of Colorado presents a complete semester graduate level course in action research on this Web site. The course syllabus, steps to be accomplished in the research process as well as relevant readings are included.

APPENDIX 4
Recommended References

Altschuld, James W., and Belle Ruth Witkin. *From Needs Assessment to Action: Transforming Needs into Solution Strategies*. Thousand Oaks, CA: Sage, 2000. This publication shows how the results of a needs assessment can be changed into action plans for an organization. It offers instructions for the procedures necessary to facilitate change.

American Association of School Librarians (AASL), and Association for Educational Communications and Technology (AECT). *Information Power: Building Partnerships for Learning*. Chicago: American Library Association, 1998.
A comprehensive and well-developed list of the nine national standards for information literacy are in the first section of the latest handbook for school library media specialists. The second section highlights the skills essential to the position of school library media specialist: collaboration, leadership, and technology.

Anderson, Gary L., Kathryn Herr, and Ann Sigrid Nihlen. *Studying Your Own School: An Educator's Guide to Qualitative Practioner Research*. Thousand Oaks, CA: Corwin Press, 1994.
This book provides an explanation of practitioner research which has the researcher as center of the process. It clarifies the differences between the various forms of inquiry including practitioner, action, and teacher research.

Booth, Wayne C., Gregory G. Colomb, and Joseph M. Williams. *The Craft of Research*. Chicago: University of Chicago Press, 1995.
   This publication is for both beginning and seasoned researchers. The authors take the researcher through all of the steps necessary in conducting a valid research product from the initial topic selection and note taking to the final paper and its presentation.

Burnaford, Gail E., Joseph Fischer, and David Hobson (Eds.). *Teachers Doing Research: The Power of Action Through Inquiry*. 2nd Ed. Mahwah, NJ: Lawrence Erlbaum Associates, 2001.
   The Editors have described the process of action research and illustrated it with examples of both experienced and apprentice teachers' action research projects.

Calhoun, Emily F. "Action Research for School Improvement." *Educational Leadership*, Mar. 2002: 18-24.
   Calhoun illustrates how action research can be used for professional development in schools by improving teaching practices. She perceives the value of action research to be through student achievement and development of leadership skills.

Farmer, Lesley S. J. *How to Conduct Action Research: A Guide for Library Media Specialists*. Chicago: AASL, 2003.
   Dr. Farmer provides an overview of the process of action research illustrating how the results of this research can be used to promote student achievement and justify the need for school library media programs.

Gustafson, Kent R., and Jane Bandy Smith. *Research for School Library Media Specialists*. Norwood, NJ: Ablex, 1994.
   This text is primarily focused on the steps to be used in conducting research. The intended audience is graduate school students participating in a research class.

Hartzell, Gary N. *Building Influence for the School Librarian*. Worthington, OH: Linworth, 1994.
   Gary N. Hartzell clarifies how important it is for school library media specialists to learn to build influence for themselves and for their libraries. Dr. Hartzell, a former high school principal, takes a business approach in helping library media specialists see how they can increase their influence in the school.

—-. *Building Influence for the School Librarian: Tenets, Targets, & Tactics*. 2nd ed. Worthington, OH: Linworth, 2003.
   Whereas the first Hartzell book concentrated on the why of building influence, Hartzell's updated version concentrates on the how. This book includes many workbook type pages and checklists to assist the school library media specialist with immediate applications.

Hubbard, Ruth S., and Brenda Power. *The Art of Classroom Inquiry: A Handbook for Teacher Researchers*. Portsmouth, NH: Heinemann, 1993.
A handbook for teacher researchers that offers directions on how to systematically develop and conduct their own personal classroom research. Practical advice on conducting studies is included.

Johnson, Andrew P. *A Short Guide to Action Research*. Rev. ed. Boston: Allyn and Bacon, 2002.
The title tells the story. This book is a simple and concise description as well as the steps to follow for a classroom teacher or administrator who would like to conduct an action research study.

Joyce, Marilyn Z. "Fostering Reading through Intrinsic Motivation: An Action Research Study." *Knowledge Quest*, Sept./Oct.: 39-40.
Marilyn Joyce shares the results of an action research study that she conducted with early adolescents on reading for understanding and enjoyment.

Lance, Keith Curry, Marcia J. Rodney, and Christine Hamilton-Pennell. *How School Librarians Help Kids Achieve Standards: The Second Colorado Study*. San Jose, CA: Hi Willow Research & Publishing, 2000.
Information and statistics presented in this research study that shows student scores on standardized tests are 10-18% higher in schools with well-funded libraries, highly qualified library media specialists with leadership qualities, and access to technological resources.

Lewin, Kurt. "Action Research and Minority Problems." *Journal of Social Issues*, Feb. 1946: 34-46.
This classic article explains the research that Kurt Lewin, "the father of action research," conducted. It shows the relationship between academic research and research conducted by a practitioner in the social science arena. Lewin uses economic and social discrimination to explain his thesis.

Martin, Janet, and Julie Tallman. "The Teacher Librarian as Action Researcher." *Teacher Librarian*, Dec. 2001.
This short article defines action research and explains the 4 basic steps that school library media specialists should follow in order to conduct this method of inquiry. The article gives specific examples of action research projects in schools which involve the school library media specialist.

Marzano, Robert J. *What Works in Schools: Translating Research into Action*. Alexandria, VA: ASCD, 2003.
Marzano relates the necessity of participating in research to enhance student achievement. He explains the factors which affect the validity of research for student success.

McArdle, Geri. *Conducting A Needs Analysis*. Menlo Park, CA: Crisp Learning, 1998. This volume is one of the Crisp 50 Minute Book Series. The quick and easy to understand guide offers a step-by-step process of needs analysis from understanding the need and identifying what should be done to developing and delivering the training necessary for results.

McLean, James E. *Improving Education Through Action Research: A Guide for Administrators and Teachers*. Thousand Oaks, CA: Corwin Press, 1995. This brief work illustrates methods for teachers and administrators to use action research as a strategy to solve problems occurring in the school arena.

McTaggart, Robin, Ed. *Participatory Action Research: International Contexts and Consequences*. New York: State University of New York Press, 1997. McTaggart collected stories of action research from numerous international authors to tell the importance of respecting "the ordinary knowledge and practice of everyday life."

Merriam, Sharan B. *Qualitative Research and Case Study Applications in Education*. Rev. and Expanded. San Francisco: Josey-Bass, 2001.
This book is designed to assist teachers and researchers in understanding qualitative research and how to formulate a qualitative study. Current case studies and advances in the field have been included to make this revised edition useful.

Mills, Geoffrey E. *Action Research: A Guide for the Teacher Researcher*. 2nd ed. Columbus OH: Merril, 2003.
Mills presents a step-by-step process into understanding the world of action research. He focuses on educational use and applications of the process stating that it is as important as assessment, curriculum development, and classroom management.

Noffke, Susan E. and Robert B. Stevensen, eds. *Educational Action Research: Becoming Practically Critical*. New York: Teachers College Press, 1995. The authors offer case studies and essays that tell about the theoretical issues of action research and discuss the problems and possible tensions that may face the researcher. This resource may be used with graduate students as well as seasoned professional educators.

Royer, Regina "Supporting Technology Integration Through Action Research." *Clearing House*. May/June 2002. EBSCO Host, 29 August 2002.
Ms. Royer addresses the problem that teachers are still reluctant to use technology for teaching and learning. She proposes that action research can be a successful staff development tool to show teachers how to use computers in the classroom.

Sagor, Richard. *Guiding School Improvement with Action Research.* Alexandria, VA: Association for Supervision and Curriculum Development, 2000.
Educators can apply the information Sagor presents in this publication. The author illustrates how instructional improvement and student success can be realized through following his clearly written step-by-step process.

—-. *How to Conduct Collaborative Action Research.* Alexandra, VA: Association for Supervision and Curriculum Development, 1992.
The 5 steps of Sagor's collaborative action research process are presented in this text. Sagor discusses how to improve the teaching and learning process through teachers' research contributions.

Schmuck, Richard A. *Practical Action Research for Change.* Arlington Heights, IL: Skylight Professional Development, 1997.
This publication offers practical steps to action research for teachers as well as administrators. Self-reflection and how to affect change are highlights of Schmuck's book which also assists the reader with understanding proactive and responsive approaches to the action research arena.

Smith Susan E., Dennis George Willms and Nancy A. Johnson, eds. *Nurtured by Knowledge: Learning to do Participatory Action-Research.* NewYork: Apex, 1997.
The authors highlight the positive effects of conducting action research on a broad scale. They explain how action research is more powerful when it involves a group with a common purpose.

Stringer, Ernest T. *Action Research.* Thousand Oaks, CA: Sage, 1999.
Ernest Stringer uses this book to describe the research tools necessary for conducting a community based action research project. The text may be used for educators as well as community or institutional organizations.

—-. *Action Research in Education.* Upper Saddle Rluer, NJ. Pearson Prentice Hall, 2003
This book is designed for novice researchers and educators interested in understanding qualitative action research. Stringer draws upon his years of field research to present information on the action research process. The text includes an entire chapter on data gathering techniques.

Sykes, Judith A. *Action Research: A Practical Guide for Transforming Your School Library.* Greenwood Village, CO: Libraries Unlimited, 2002.
A monograph of Ms. Sykes action research project is presented in this publication. The second part is a power point presentation that librarians might use to inform administrators or the public of their role in the educational arena.

Viadero, D. "Holding Up a Mirror." *Education Week*, 12 June 2002: 32+.
    The article tells Diane Painter's story of using teacher research for improvement of professional practice in Fairfax County Schools in Virginia. Colleague-based research groups and increased focus on student success are further highlights that make this article useful to teachers, community, and administrators.

Weir, Peter. *Dead Poet's Society*. Touchstone, 1989.
    This Disney Touchstone production is story of John Keating, an inspiring teacher at Welton Academy for boys. Robin Williams offers a memorable performance as he broadens his students' awareness of the possibilities of life through a connection with literature.

Wolcott, Harry F. *A Kwakiutl Village and School*. New York: Holt, Rinehart and Winston, 1967.
    An anthropological case study of two forms of children's education on an island off Vancouver Island. Wolcott discusses the study through the eyes of a participant observer.

—-. *Writing Up Qualitative Research*. London: Sage, 1990.
    Wolcott wrote this book as a revision to an earlier work outlining methods of research. He offers straight- forward instructions on how to begin a project, methods of putting things together, and how to publish the findings.

WORKS CITED

American Association of School Librarians (AASL), and Association for Educational Communications and Technology (AECT). *Information Power: Building Partnerships for Learning*. Chicago: American Library Association, 1998.

Booth, Wayne C., Gregory G. Colomb, and Joseph M. Williams. *The Craft of Research*. Chicago: University of Chicago Press, 1995.

Farmer, Lesley S. J. *How to Conduct Action Research: A Guide for Library Media Specialists*. Chicago: AASL, 2003.

Gustafson, Kent R., and Jane Bandy Smith. *Research for School Library Media Specialists*. Norwood, NJ: Ablex, 1994.

Hartzell, Gary. *Building Influence for the School Librarian*. Worthington, OH: Linworth, 1994.

—-. *Building Influence for the School Librarian: Tenets, Targets, & Tactics*. 2nd ed. Worthington, OH: Linworth, 2003.

Hubbard, Ruth S., and Brenda Power. *The Art of Classroom Inquiry: A Handbook for Teacher Researchers*. Portsmouth, NH: Heinemann, 1993.

Johnson, Andrew P. *A Short Guide to Action Research*. Rev. ed. Boston: Allyn and Bacon, 2002.

Joyce, Marilyn Z. "Fostering Reading through Intrinsic Motivation: An Action Research Study." *Knowledge Quest*, Sept./Oct.: 39-40.

Lance, Keith Curry, Marcia J. Rodney, and Christine Hamilton-Pennell. *How School Librarians Help Kids Achieve Standards: The Second Colorado Study*. San Jose, CA: Hi Willow Research & Publishing, 2000.

Lewin, Kurt. "Action Research and Minority Problems." *Journal of Social Issues*, Feb. 1946: 34-46.

Mills, Geoffrey E. *Action Research: A Guide for the Teacher Researcher*. 2nd ed. Columbus OH: Merril, 2003.

Sagor, Richard. *Guiding School Improvement With Action Research*. Alexandria, VA: Association for Supervision and Curriculum Development, 2000.

—-. *How to Conduct Collaborative Action Research*. Alexandra, VA: Association for Supervision and Curriculum Development, 1992.

Schmuck, Richard A. *Practical Action Research for Change*. Arlington Heights, IL: Skylight Professional Development, 1997.

GLOSSSARY

Accountability – a method by which schools and school districts evaluate themselves by examining their academic achievement, standards, and assessments.

Action research – a reflective method of problem solving where the researcher develops specific solutions to specific problems.

Affective questions – a strategy for questioning which elicits responses including the subject's attitudes, values, or feelings.

Archival sources – stored records or data which are maintained by an agency that tracks community, student, and staff patterns.

Attitudinal questions – a strategy for questioning which elicits responses relating to values and trustworthiness.

Best practices – instructional methods and strategies that provide examples of quality work.

Coding (codified) data – a method or scheme of grouping data into sets or groups to classify and clarify information.

Cognitive questions – a strategy for questioning which elicits higher-level thinking responses, needing full understanding of the meaning of the topic.

Confidence interval – the number used to estimate the likely size of a population parameter. The interval gives an estimated range of values calculated from a given set of sample data.

Confidence level – the calculated number which tells how the answers from the sample population may be interpreted for the entire population.

Control group – the samples in a study that do not have the variable introduced to affect change.

Collaborate – a method of teaching or working together in which team members complement others' knowledge, talents, and expertise.

Disaggregate – a method of separating data or statistics into groups and sub-sets to further define the item being studied.

ERIC (Educational Resources Information Center) – a database containing journals and research reports on many subjects in the educational field. ERIC is accessible through print, microfiche, or online.

Ethics – guiding values, standards, or principles.

Experimental group – the sample of subjects, classes, or participants who have a variable introduced to affect change.

Flow chart – a diagram that shows step-by-step progression through a process or system by using special symbols and connecting lines.

Flexible schedule – the method of organizing the availability of library media center resources throughout the school day so that students may utilize and check out materials as needed. The library media specialist's time is utilized for the learning and teaching needs of students and staff.

Generalizability – the attribute of research that provides for the replication of the research project in more than one location with the same or similar results.

Graphic organizer – a tool developed to assist in recording and organizing related information (matrix, chart, or rubric).

Inductive analysis – reasoning from particular examples to a general conclusion.

Information literacy standards – nine national standards for student success, which align with content standards developed by AASL and AECT.

Information Power: Building Partnerships for Learning – a publication that sets the guidelines for developing the school library media program and teaching information literacy standards. The book was developed jointly by AASL and AECT and published in 1998.

Interviews – a method of collecting data by asking specific questions in a face-to-face scripted setting. This method allows the interviewer to establish a comfortable rapport with the interviewee.

Journaling – a method of collecting data through personal reflections in an expository form. This method allows the researcher to record significant insights.

Literature matrix – a method of visually representing the professional materials relating to a specific topic.

Observations – a method of collecting data by watching events occur either through active or passive participation.

Online database – a computerized file of periodical indexes. Libraries gain access to this material through a subscription service.

Peer review – a method of sharing thoughts, ideas, plans, and results with professional colleagues to ascertain the feasibility and validity of the action research project.

Personal bias – beliefs that are influenced by ethnicity, culture, gender, or religion.

Proactive action research – implementing a new practice to solve a problem which is then analyzed through conducting action research.

Quantitative data – findings which can be analyzed through counting specific results.

Qualitative data – findings which are descriptive in nature rather than numerical.

Questionnaires – printed survey instruments that may be used to tabulate and analyze results or findings.

Random sample – a representative part of the population, each having an equal chance of being selected.

Reflective practice – the art of analyzing one's professional situation to determine the path or steps for improvement.

Reliability – the extent to which an experiment, test, or measuring procedure yields the same results through repeated trials.

Sustained Silent Reading – a method whereby students and staff dedicate a certain amount of time each day or week simultaneously for personal reading, often known as SSR.

Specials rotation – a method that some elementary and middle schools employ in scheduling classes using subjects such as art, physical education, computers, music, and sometimes the library, in order to provide the classroom teachers with planning time.

Triangulate – the process of using at least three data collection methods to determine the validity and reliability of the information.

Validity – a method of determining the truthfulness of a basic premise.

Variable – a quality that can assume any one of a set of values.

INDEX

Action Research and Minority Problems 3, 101, 106
Affective questions 107
AltaVista 14
American Association of School Librarians (AASL) 1, 24, 70, 99, 105
Archival sources 36, 44, 107
The Art of Classroom Inquiry 32, 101, 105
Association for Educational Communications and Technology (AECT) 1, 24, 99, 105
Attitudinal questions 107
Best practices 11, 107
Building Influence for the School Librarian 70, 100, 105
Booth, Wayne C. 9, 100, 105
Coalition of Essential Schools 23
Coding the data xi, 51, 56
Cognitive questions 107
Collaborate *ix*, 2, 4, 34, 55, 58, 91, 108
Colomb, Gregory G. 9, 100, 105
Computer platform 12
Computer lab 12, 30, 31, 33, 39, 81-93
Confidence interval 47, 107
Confidence level 47, 107
The Craft of Research 9, 100, 105
Dead Poet's Society 30, 104
Disaggregated data 37, 44, 108
ERIC 14, 108
Ethics 33, 47-48, 50, 108
Farmer, Lesley S. J. 2, 9, 12, 30, 46, 84, 93, 100, 105
Flow chart 30, 108
Flexible schedule *ix*, 7, 11-12, 16, 32-34, 44, 50, 55, 58-59, 62, 81-93, 108
Fostering Reading through Intrinsic Motivation 12, 101, 105
Generalizability 45, 50, 108

Google 14
Graphic organizer 15-17, 108
Guiding School Improvement with Action Research 9, 30, 35, 36, 40, 42, 46, 54, 58, 103, 106
Gustafson, Kent R. 30, 51, 100, 105
Hamilton-Pennell, Christine 101, 106
Hartzell, Gary 70, 100, 105
How School Librarians Help Kids Achieve Standards 101, 106
How to Conduct Action Research 2, 9, 12, 30, 35, 46, 54, 100, 105
How to Conduct Collaborative Action Research 30, 103, 106
Hubbard, Ruth S. 32, 101, 105
Inductive analysis 54, 108
Interviews 44, 46, 48-49, 54, 62, 109
Information literacy standards 3, 12, 15, 24, 34, 58, 61-62, 91, 108
Information Power ix, 1, 24, 65, 75, 99, 105, 108
Interlibrary loan 14, 16-17
Johnson, Andrew P. 6, 35, 49-50, 54, 58, 101, 105
Journaling 10, 12, 49, 81-93, 109
Joyce, M. Z. 12, 101, 105
Lance, Keith Curry 45, 84, 87, 101, 106
Lewin, Kurt 3, 101, 106
Library automation system 12, 32, 42, 86
Literature matrix 15, 109
Mills, Geoffrey E. 2, 4, 6, 9, 15, 35, 42, 58, 61, 102, 106
Observations 36, 42-44, 49, 53-55, 59, 62, 86, 109
Online database 14, 32-34, 42, 53, 59, 84, 87, 90, 109
Peer review 49, 109

Personal bias 47, 50, 109
Power, Brenda 32, 101, 105
Practical Action Research for Change 6, 103, 106
Proactive action research 6, 48, 109
Quantitative data 5, 32, 51, 54, 56, 109
Qualitative data 4-5, 32, 51-53, 56, 109
Questionnaires 36-38, 40-41, 44, 48, 88, 91, 109
Reliability 5, 7, 35, 45-47, 50, 51-52, 66, 109, 110
Research for School Library Media Specialists 30, 51, 100, 105
Rodney, Marcia J. 101, 106
Sagor, Richard 9, 11, 30, 35-36, 40, 42, 46, 54, 58, 103, 106
Schmuck, Richard A. 4, 6, 35, 38, 41, 43, 48, 103, 106
Second language students 12
A Short Guide to Action Research 6, 35, 49-50, 54, 58, 101, 105
Sizer, Theodore 23
Smith, Jane Bandy 30, 51, 100, 105
Sustained Silent Reading 12, 31, 33, 109
Technology specialist 12, 30-31, 33
Triangulate 35, 52, 110
Triangulation 35, 49, 56, 59, 66, 68, 74, 81, 86, 88
Validity 5, 7, 11, 14, 35, 45-47, 50, 51, 66, 101, 109, 110
Variable 3-4, 15, 46, 108, 110
Visual representation 6, 15-16, 30, 37, 54, 58
Weir, Peter 104
Williams, Joseph M. 9, 100, 105
Williams, Robin 30, 104
Wireless technology 12
Yahoo 14

ABOUT THE AUTHORS

Jody Howard is the Manager of the School Library Masters and Endorsement Program at the University of Colorado at Denver. For the past 4 years, she Co-Coordinated the Program. Prior to this, Jody worked 20 years in Adams County Five Star schools as a classroom teacher and a school librarian in grades K-12. Between 1999-2004, Jody was the District Library Coordinator for Adams12. Jody has co-authored articles in various library-related areas including collaboration and intellectual freedom. She has served on state and national legislative and intellectual freedom committees and presented at numerous conferences and workshops.

Su Eckhardt has experience teaching in all grade levels and many subjects, starting her career as an elementary classroom teacher. She has worked at various rural and metropolitan schools in Colorado. For the past 18 years she has been with Cherry Creek School District in south suburban Denver. She was Library Coordinator at Smoky Hill High School for 15 years. Highlights of her high school career include being recognized with the AASL SLMPY Award in 1995. Su co-authored *Teaching Internet Basics*, a guide for library media specialist instruction. She has presented at numerous state and national conferences and workshops. She currently works as the District Teacher Librarian for Cherry Creek and is a graduate instructor for the University of Colorado at Denver in the school library program.

CPSIA information can be obtained
at www.ICGtesting.com
Printed in the USA
BVHW022357270423
663204BV00013B/165